Y0-FCS-145

Thinking about the curriculum

Thinking about the curriculum

The nature and treatment of curriculum problems

William A. Reid

Routledge & Kegan Paul
London, Henley and Boston

50754

First published in 1978
by Routledge & Kegan Paul Ltd
39 Store Street,
London WC1E 7DD,
Broadway House,
Newtown Road,
Henley-on-Thames,
Oxon RG9 1EN and
9 Park Street,
Boston, Mass. 02108, USA
Set in Times by
Computacomp (UK) Ltd, Fort William, Scotland
and printed in Great Britain by
Lowe & Brydone Printers Ltd, Thetford, Norfolk
© William A. Reid 1978
No part of this book may be reproduced in any form without permission from the publisher, except for the quotation of brief passages in criticism

British Library Cataloguing in Publication Data

Reid, William Arbuckle

Thinking about the curriculum.
1. Education – Curricula
I. Title
375 LB1570 78–40461

ISBN 0–7100–8979–1
ISBN 0–7100–8980–5 Pbk.

Contents

50754

Illustrations

Figures

Tables

Preface

The problems of the field of Curriculum Studies are becoming, and in my view should become, the problems of the community at large. The essays in this book argue that the field should reorientate itself to develop a view of curriculum that sees it as the possession of communities and not of professionals and initiates. To do this, it has to find for itself an identity that avoids alliances with technocrats, bureaucrats or ideologues, but yet has a positive philosophy and a commitment to values. The view put forward here is that it should do this, not in a purely theoretic way, but keeping as its central concern a consideration of how the practical tasks of curriculum-planning, implementing and evaluating are to be carried out. The book is aimed at all those, whether in the 'curriculum field' or not, who are challenged by the practical and intellectual difficulties of defining the nature of curriculum problems and finding solutions to them.

It would not have been written without the help and inspiration of many people. I am greatly indebted to Wendy Hughes whose assistance in the preparation of the typescript was indispensable, and to colleagues and students in the Birmingham Faculty of Education who in conversation and seminars have given me the benefit of their experience and of their insights into curriculum problems. My thanks for helpful criticism and stimulation to try new ways of thinking about curriculum issues are especially due to Ian Westbury of the University of Illinois, Elliot Eisner and Decker Walker of Stanford University, William Lowe and William Pinar of the University of Rochester, David Hamilton of the University of East Anglia and Philip Taylor of the University of Birmingham.

Birmingham William A. Reid

1 Introduction: Curriculum debates and Curriculum Studies

> In his speech at Ruskin College ... the Prime Minister called for a public debate on education. The debate was not to be confined to those professionally concerned with education, but was to give full opportunity for employers and trades unions, and parents, as well as teachers and administrators, to make their views known. (*Education in Schools: A Consultative Document*, Cmnd 6869, London, HMSO, 1977, p.2)

> There are many different voices but little joining of these voices in a give-and-take exchange. It is a mistake to think of this cacophony as a debate; there is little opportunity to listen and to formulate thoughtful response. ... The claims and charges are often so contradictory or mutually exclusive that one is led to wonder what actually goes on in schools, whether generalisations are possible and whether anybody knows. (NIE Curriculum Development Task Force, *Current Issues, Problems, and Concerns in Curriculum Development*, Report to NCER, 1976, p. 4)

The 1970s are the decade of curriculum crisis: what could previously be left to the bureaucrats and the professionals is now a matter of acute public concern. Partly this is because schools have been too successful in their claims on economic resources. 'Quite suddenly ... the schools lost their status as sacred cows. Driven by Sputnik, racial conflict, and new frontiers, the school bubble had outgrown all non-military budgets and had burst.'[1] And partly it is because the curriculum – what the school is there to provide – has lost touch with the wants of individuals and the needs of the community. In our concern to lavish more resources on educational systems, to bring more of their benefits to more people, we had lost the ability to reflect on fundamental purposes, to match technical efficiency with quality of learning and professional commitment with public service. Now crisis is creating a new arena for the resolution of curriculum problems. An arena which will offer new roles to public and to professionals alike. But to invite public discussion and debate is one thing. To see what kind of a debate is relevant to curriculum problems and to provide the situations and the skills that enable it to be adequately conducted is another. And for the professional – the teacher, the administrator or researcher – who must review his expertise and commitment, where are the appropriate models, concepts or ideals that should guide his reorientation? These are issues that everyone must be concerned about; they are of central importance to all those who through teaching or research or as students are members of the academic field of Curriculum Studies.

The essays in this book relate to various aspects of these problems. They identify and discuss what seem to me to be the important themes that we should be concerned with as a necessary preliminary step to tackling curriculum questions through the arena of public policy-making rather than through the closed world of the initiate and the expert.

First of all, if we are, as a community, to try to find answers to curriculum problems, we have to think about them, and that, in turn, means identifying the kinds of thinking that are appropriate to them. Is it just the application of common sense that is needed? Or should we try to 'think' in the sense of applying concepts or theories? Is there any justice in the argument that the curriculum is something realised in action, something 'practical' that cannot be made the subject of theory?

If debate should be informed by intelligence[2] about the present state of the school curriculum and about the possibilities that exist for change and how change can be brought about, what kinds of enquiry should be undertaken to produce this intelligence? What kind of a concept of curriculum research should we have? Obviously, our answer to this question depends on whether we conceive of curriculum as something that demands practical or theoretic styles of thinking, or some mixture of the two.

How should thought and intelligence actually be applied to curriculum problems? Can the debate be conducted in a purely procedural way? Can we from known premises reach sure conclusions? How should questions of ends and means be treated in discussion on the curriculum? How do value questions and moral principles enter into it? This is the arena in which reorientation is perhaps most urgently needed. Our preoccupation with the 'what' question distracts our attention from the even more important 'how' questions that go along with it. 'What should be taught in schools?' or 'What should students learn?' are not problems that can be solved simply by applying thought and intelligence in some kind of abstract way. The thought and intelligence have to be applied by people who work through social, administrative or political structures. Unless we can provide adequate answers to questions of how this should be done, no amount of effort in other directions will produce better curriculum decisions.

Curricula are provided through organisations. If we are to make good decisions about ways in which curricula should be changed we have to understand the nature of these organisations, the circumstances under which they may be open to change and those under which they will resist it; what they are capable of doing and what they cannot achieve, however much we would like them to. In the absence of such an understanding debates on the content or purposes of the curriculum risk being purely ritualistic exercises.

Finally, what are the general implications for Curriculum Studies of the approaches to curriculum problems suggested in the earlier essays? What kind of an identity should it be seeking and what kinds of leading metaphors should guide its enquiries? Faced with a variety of possible futures, which should we choose and what are the criteria which should determine our preferences?

The essays, then, relate to two major and interconnected concerns: how can communities adequately debate questions of curricular ends and means, and how can Curriculum Studies be conceived as an enquiry that assists in the resolution of curriculum problems?

Deliberation as a means of solving curriculum problems

Throughout the essays the word 'deliberation' is preferred to the word 'debate'. The reasons for this are, first, that deliberation is a more narrowly defined term and a more appropriate one, so it is argued,[3] for debates on the curriculum. Second, the word has been used already by curriculum writers who have made considerable contributions to a literature defining and elaborating on it.[4] Third, there is a need to set new directions, to turn away from the connotations of the word 'debate' and to think anew about what is needed when specifically curriculum problems are at issue: what contexts and situations, what styles of argument and reasoning. In places, especially in Chapter 4, the way curriculum 'debates' are currently conducted is explicitly criticised. In others it is criticised by implication. Those criticisms may be summarised as follows:

1 Debate proceeds on the assumption that schools and school systems are rational institutions, and that their behaviour can be changed by giving them appropriate instructions.
2 The schools' capacity to deliver on goals is not questioned. If some predetermined level of competency is to be required of students, then it is just a matter of instituting the necessary tests to check that it has been achieved.
3 Schools and communities are thought of as uniform. Throughout a country or a state, they can be subject to the same policies.
4 Though much play is made with the word 'debate', education and

decision-making on education are thought of as happening within relatively closed systems.

5 Fundamental questions of curricular purposes are pushed on one side. Especially, the moral nature of curriculum decision-making is passed over.

6 Discussion is imbued with a commitment to 'right answerism'[5] – a belief that problems can be solved in some final sense through the discovery of the right formula.

7 There is a low level of emphasis on data. It is thought that what happens in schools is a matter of common knowledge or can be found out by asking people who 'know'.

8 Questions of how to arrive at decisions are thought of as relatively unimportant (or, again, as 'something we all know') compared to questions of what should be taught and learned.

The 'debate' launched in England by the Prime Minister's Ruskin College speech in 1976 showed all these characteristics. The speech was based on an unpublished policy document produced within the Department of Education and Science and known as the Yellow Book. Some of its contents are known through the printing of extensive pirated extracts in the *Times Educational Supplement*[6] (subsequent references to Yellow Book are to the *TES* article). It deals with four 'problems':

> the issue of the basic approach to teaching the 3 Rs in primary schools; the curricula for older children in comprehensive schools; the examination system; the general problems of 16 to 19 year olds who had no prospect of going on directly to higher education.[7]

Obviously, these are exceedingly ill-defined 'problems'. The first might sound as though it were reasonably limited in scope, but then that impression is dispelled by referring to it as an 'issue' rather than a 'problem'. These are, in fact, general curricular areas about which there are more or less articulated feelings of unease. A great deal of work would need to be done before those feelings could lead to the identification of specific problems that one might set out to solve. The treatment of the 'issues' in the Yellow Book may be exemplified by studying what it has to say about the curricula of secondary comprehensive schools. First a range of criticisms is reviewed: there is 'a feeling that the schools have become too easy going ... some employers complain that school leavers cannot express themselves clearly and lack the basic mathematical skills'; students may be permitted 'to choose unbalanced or not particularly profitable curricula' and there are 'pressures from a variety of specialised lobbies for the secondary curriculum to embrace their particular aims'.[8] An appropriate next step might have been to try to formulate the criticisms in more specific ways and review data that might assist in evaluating them. Alternatively, if data are lacking, to suggest what might be done to obtain them. What do employers mean by 'express themselves clearly' or 'basic mathematical skills'? In what ways are deficiencies in these areas thought to be a problem? Which employers are worried? Given a better insight into what is causing concern, what statistics or what research evidence can help decide whether the concern is justified? But the discussion does not proceed in this way. Rather it assumes the worries to be well founded and puts up speculative theories about how the problems may have been caused. 'In an almost desperate attempt to modify styles of teaching and learning so as to capture the imagination and enlist the cooperation of their more difficult pupils, some [teachers] have possibly been too ready to drop their sights in setting standards of performance', and 'Some teachers and some schools may have overemphasised the importance of preparing boys and girls for their roles in society compared with the need to prepare them for their economic role'.[9] Logically, of course, speculation about how problems arise is quite beside the point at a stage when the problems have yet to be defined and evidence considered on the extent to which they are real or imaginary. This further discussion seems rather to fulfil the function of clinching rumour by innuendo (curiously, the repeated 'possiblys' and 'may haves' seem almost to reinforce the indictment by implying that kindness forbids the telling of the plain truth, rather than soften it by admitting the lack of foundation for the points that are being made).[10] The next step (still in advance of the identification of the problems) is to propose solutions: 'The time has probably come to try to establish generally accepted principles for the composition of the secondary curriculum for all pupils, that is to say a "core curriculum".' The equation of 'generally accepted principles' with 'core curriculum' is, of course, a further logical fallacy.[11]

However, the document was only the first step in initiating a political process intended to lead to curriculum reform. Following the official announcement of public discussion (the expression 'great debate' was in common currency even before the prime ministerial announcement) further papers were produced which attempted to set out 'agendas'. These elaborated on the curriculum issues of the 'Yellow Book'. That is, they concentrated on the 'what' questions. 'How' one has a debate on curriculum issues was not a topic for discussion, in spite of the fact that, as this was the first occasion for many years that public participation in the consideration of the school curriculum had been invited, it could hardly be claimed that there was a well-established tradition of how such things should be managed. It seems to have been assumed that the pattern of debate would be of the type commonly associated with legislative assemblies. The gatherings would be large, most participants would be 'representing' someone or something, and contributions would be limited to one or two statements per person. Eight regional one-day meetings were to be organised in the spring of 1977. The 'background paper' which was prepared, referred to here as *Educating our Children*,[12] showed some consciousness that this kind of debate might not be able to make much progress on solving all our curriculum problems:

> In a conference lasting one day, only a limited number of issues can be discussed profitably. ... (F)our main topics have been chosen for debate. These are:
>
> (a) the curriculum;
> (b) the assessment of standards;
> (c) the education and training of teachers;
> (d) school and working life.[13]

At that rate of progress, maybe two days of conference *would* have solved all our problems? One wonders why such a small extra investment was not made.

Educating our Children was, however, the product of a 'first stage' of debate consisting of 'preliminary meetings with a limited number of educational and industrial organisations, at which a paper outlining possible issues for consideration was discussed'. (This paper will be referred to as the 'Annotated Agenda'.[14]) So perhaps within the general area of, for example, 'the curriculum' it was specific problems which the conferences were to discuss, derived through stage one from the general issues?

There is, as far as I know, no reliable published source for what happened in this preliminary stage of the 'debate'. To judge how effective it was in advancing the discussion of curriculum problems, all one can do is compare the sequence of documents from the Yellow Book through the Annotated Agenda to *Educating our Children* to see in what ways argument and evidence have been used, or how far new possibilities have been considered or new views sought and taken into account. The Annotated Agenda states that it is designed to 'encourage a fresh look at the problems, the paper therefore avoids a comprehensive review of existing policies and intentions'.[15] In fact, after a one-page introduction, a heading 'Curriculum' is followed immediately by a paragraph entitled 'Common Core Curriculum' which asks, 'Would a "common core" curriculum be a solution?' Those who would like to know in any detail to what it is supposed to be a solution, presumably have to consult the (unpublished) Yellow Book and that, as we have seen, deals with the question in a very sketchy way. Under a separate heading 'Monitoring/Assessment' a further solution to curriculum problems is put forward which was only briefly hinted at in the Yellow Book. 'Is there a case for tests in English language and mathematics to be taken by all pupils ... at certain ages, possibly 8, 11 and 13?'[16] A sentence at the head of the section states: 'The Assessment of

Performance Unit (APU) has been set up within DES to develop tests which can be used to monitor the performance of the system as a whole'.[17] Here, then, is a difference between the first and the second publications, but one which relates to a solution already being implemented rather than something that has emerged from further reflection or gathering of evidence. *Educating our Children*, as might be expected, is somewhat further removed from the Yellow Book in content and format than is the Annotated Agenda. However, the pedigree of the document is plain to see. The same 'anxieties' over the curriculum are rehearsed again, though in a different order, and the notion of a 'common core curriculum' immediately introduced with the statement that 'A good deal of the debate centres around the need for [it]'.[18] What is meant here by 'debate' we are not told. Is this a hint of what happened in stage one? If so, it is singularly inexplicit. Or is it a hint of what the writers of the Agenda would like to happen at stage two? There follows a brief discussion of possible different interpretations of 'common core' ending with the statement that 'It may be useful first to consider what schools do'.[19] For secondary schools, this consists of a page or so outlining a 'common knowledge' statement about how, in general, the curriculum is organised. For example:

> In the fourth and fifth years, when the programme for most pupils covers some eight or nine subjects, the fixed points in the curriculum in current practice are likely to be no more than four: English, mathematics, religious education and physical education. To this should be added careers education and guidance. Many schools attempt to add a science and, less often, a foreign language for most of their pupils.[20]

This is hardly in the nature of firm evidence about what schools do. What are we to understand by the last sentence quoted? How many is 'many'? or 'most'? And how is 'attempting' to add a science different from adding it?

More movement is shown on the question of the assessment of standards. The corresponding section in *Educating our Children* speaks of 'assessment by sampling' rather than checking on the 'standards' reached by individuals or by schools which was the kind of emphasis which the Annotated Agenda seemed to be making.[21] Here may be some acknowledgment of the paucity of evidence to support claims that standards have fallen and that arguments based on that premise are hard to sustain. 'There is little quantitative national evidence of trends in educational standards except for the national reading surveys carried out since 1948. The most recently published results were from the 1970 survey and subject to a wide margin of error.' But, 'The fact that there is widespread feeling that standards need to be raised cannot be ignored.'[22] The main change through the series of documents seems to be that the focus on solutions, rather than problems, has been sharpened. The solutions are the ones originally proposed in the Yellow Book, but in a slightly redefined form. This is clear from the two-and-a-half page duplicated set of questions for discussion at the regional conferences. The section on 'Curriculum' states:

> The fundamental requirement is to meet the needs and reasonable aspirations of pupils and the needs of the country. The problem is to ensure the coverage of certain essentials without stifling the initiatives of teachers, preventing innovation or making education unduly narrow.
>
> Two major questions arise:
>
> i What should be the aims and content of a core curriculum?
> ii How best can an agreed core curriculum be put into effect?

The general conclusion must be that the role of the 'stage one' debate in clarifying the issues preparatory to stage two was very muted. What seems to have happened is that preconceived proposals, such as those for a 'core curriculum' or for testing of basic competencies, were aired to see what kind of support or opposition they met and whether it would be politically wise to modify them in some way, or whether clarifications of one kind or another would be helpful in getting support for them.

Yet it is known that there were, even within the fairly narrow range of those 'educational and industrial organisations' who were to be consulted in stage one, some different views about the identification of the problems and what should be done about them. For example, towards the end of 1976, the Rubber and Plastics Industry Training Board produced a report which blamed 'the influence of the universities and of the exam system for an unchanging curriculum which is too academic for most pupils' needs', and called for 'an approach based on a range of "alternative curricular pathways" which will provide a survival kit for modern living'. The report also stressed the need to 'involve groups from outside teaching in the planning and implementation of the new curricula'.[23] There is no sign in *Educating our Children* that such things were even being thought about, let alone that they might make a serious contribution to a debate on needed improvements in the school curriculum.

The conferences followed a predictable pattern, as did the unofficial television and radio 'debates' which went on alongside them. Well-known positions were reiterated by representatives of various interested parties, or by adherents of known orthodoxies of one kind or another. Evidence to support views put forward continued to be scarce, and, where it conflicted with predetermined positions, was generally discounted on some *ad hoc* grounds which cast doubt on its reliability or enabled it to be explained away. Where it seemed to support a position it was liable to be accepted with a total lack of critical examination.[24] Following on the conferences a Green Paper[25] was laid before Parliament by the Secretary of State for Education and Science in July 1977. Again, an opportunity exists to see how far and in what directions the understanding of curricular problems and their solutions had been moved on as a result of 'debate'.

If a reader were presented with extracts from the Green Paper alongside parallel passages from the preceding documents, he would be hard put to it to identify which were which. In some ways the language is closer to that of the Yellow Book than that of *Educating our Children*. For example, the phrase 'The time has probably come to establish generally accepted principles for the composition of the secondary curriculum for all pupils' is echoed in 'It is clear that the time has come to try to establish generally acceptable principles for the composition of the secondary curriculum for all pupils'.[26] The 'debate' seems to have served as a background to the DES's attempt to redraft the same paper three times in the course of a year. Occasionally tones of voice have been penetrative enough to persuade the redrafters to lean in this direction or that, but the completion of the exercise is marked, not by the discovery of things we did not know, or the arrival of new insights or understandings, but by the feeling that the opportunity has arrived to delete 'The time has probably come' and substitute 'It is clear that the time has come'. Sadly, the 'debate' is considered closed, and authority over the curriculum has been gathered back into the closed circle of the most interested parties:

> It would not be compatible with the duty of the Secretary of State to 'promote the education of the people of England and Wales', or with their accountability to Parliament, to abdicate from leadership on educational issues which have become a matter of lively public concern. The Secretaries of State will therefore seek to establish a broad agreement with their partners in the education service on a framework for the curriculum, and, particularly, on whether, because there are aims common to all schools and to all pupils at certain stages, there should be a 'core' or 'protected part'.[27]

Not found wanting because it was never tried should be the verdict on the debate.

> The most persistent complaint of witnesses was that the DES does not consult sufficiently with interested parties before reaching policy decisions. The Department's representatives, however, clearly believed that they consulted as fully as they reasonably could and that they had 'an open door'. From the evidence it is clear that 'consultation' or 'participation' mean different things to different people.[28]

The contribution of Curriculum Studies

The term 'curriculum crisis' has not been used lightly. Many signs point to the fact that the curriculum problems we face today are fundamental ones, not to be treated as 'operating problems' or questions of improving what is already good. Curriculum Studies is a field of enquiry which claims to provide insights into the nature of the school curriculum (to use a minimal definition to which, presumably, theorists and researchers of differing views would all subscribe); what should its response be to a situation where established authorities are losing touch with the needs of communities and individuals, where purposes and structures are out of harmony, where the skills needed to relate means to ends and norms to ideals seem to have been lost and where questions of what should be taught and learned are as much moral and ethical in character as technical and organisational? What kind of philosophy should guide its search for an academic identity and its involvement with the practicalities of designing, implementing and evaluating curricula? The two approaches which seem to dominate current writing in Curriculum Studies are poorly equipped to inspire the kinds of research and theorising that the situation calls for. The first of these approaches is what I would call the 'rational managerial'.[29] This concentrates on producing methodologies for carrying out curriculum tasks – design, implementation, evaluation – which depend on the identification of procedures following rules variously described as 'rational', 'scientific' or 'logical'. Writers in this tradition speak of objectives, often of behavioural objectives, of psychometric methods for curriculum evaluation, of educational technology, of systems theory and of mastery learning. They are concerned with the technical apparatus of curricular activities, with control and efficiency, with performance and goal achievement. Questions of broad purpose, of morality, of *whose* goals are to be pursued with efficiency are left on one side. The second approach is what I would call that of the 'radical critique'. The theorist is aware of problems of 'hidden curricula' of purposes and processes that lie behind calls for the achievement of objectives or for the extension of the claims of systems over individuals. But his response is either to remove himself to a higher moral and intellectual plane from which he can safely criticise those who actually get involved in practical curriculum tasks, or to declare that the only way of being involved in the improvement of curricula is to work for social revolution (usually in a Marxist sense). A third approach is offered by what might be termed 'popular' rather than 'academic' curriculum writing. This is what could be labelled the 'reactionary' solution. Things were good in the past, so let's try to recreate the satisfactory features of the system that we have lost, or re-establish the desirable goals we think are being neglected. This is the flavour of much of the writing of the series of Black Papers[30] published in England over the last few years, and indeed of the various drafts of the DES document calling for a core curriculum and an emphasis on the teaching and testing of basic skills. It is also traceable in state legislation in the United States on minimal competency testing and in state court decisions on the duty of public education systems to teach basic skills.

The three approaches are comparable to the three responses to 'loss of the stable state' described by Schon.[31] Where curriculum thinking extends simply to the refurbishing and renewal of courses within existing frameworks of aims and objectives, the 'rational managerial' view has its usefulness. (This was the case at the time of the curriculum reform movements of the 1960s which were confident and expansionist in character.) But in an epoch when doubt is cast on the fundamental purposes of education and the curriculum, a 'rational managerial' approach is equivalent to Schon's category of 'mindlessness':

> This is an attempt to escape from anguish and uncertainty by evading reflective consciousness itself. The methods may be drugs, hypnotic routine, violence, or a peculiar union with machine technology – like the kids in mid-western American towns who tool around empty squares at night on motorcycles or in hot rods and seem to be saying, 'The machine is winning. Why not join it?'[32]

The 'radical critique' takes various forms, but often seems close to the second possibility – 'Revolt' – 'a form of revolutionary response whose warcry is total rejection of the past and of all vestiges of the past in existing social systems'.[33] 'Reaction' corresponds to 'Return', a nostalgic seeking after a previous and often imaginary or at least romanticised 'stable state', oblivious of the fact that the world has moved on and that the conditions that gave it stability no longer obtain.

Reaction and revolt are opposite faces of the same thing. Both are authoritarian attempts to solve society's problems. Both know the answers to current dilemmas even before they have been articulated. In the one case the object of the authoritarian action is the achievement of an imaginary state of affairs that existed in the past; in the other of an equally imaginary state of affairs that, it is believed, will exist in the future. Neither school of thought allows that problems and solutions have to be looked for and discovered, and that where these affect whole communities, the act of discovery is one in which the community should be involved. To allow such a thing is to allow that the community might see other problems and other solutions than the reactionaries or the revolutionaries might be comfortable with. Neither group, for example, seems to be able to view with equanimity the idea that curricular purposes could be achieved other than through schools. In the case of the reactionary, this is easily understandable. The past state of affairs after which he hankers was achieved by schooling, so schooling must be a necessary element in its re-establishment. But why should the revolutionary be so attached to schools? On reading some 'radically' inspired articles and books one wonders. Vague feelings of unease with people like Illich are expressed, without the reason for the unease ever becoming clear.[34] But then, in other places, the cause of the anxiety surfaces with some clarity: 'An open attempt to subvert bourgeois schools will make central the question of *control* of educational power – a socialist party must use what power it can get.'[35] For those who consider themselves to have superior vision to others, and for whom the vision is of some already revealed truth, institutions are essential as a means of imposing their views. The closeness of the two types of authoritarian attitude to the school curriculum is well expressed by Gretton and Jackson in their analysis of the 'William Tyndale' affair. Speaking of the methods adopted by the 'radical' teachers, they comment:

> The assumptions have not changed ... the teacher is still wanting the parents to commit their children unreservedly to him. ... No allowance is made for any diversity of views among parents, nor even for any expression of any views which might be allowed to influence the teachers.[36]

If against reaction and revolt we can set only a 'rational managerial' approach to curriculum theory and research, then the capacity of Curriculum Studies to treat its practical and theoretic problems is weak indeed. For this tradition cannot speak to curriculum issues that involve the resolution of moral questions, or decide on competing claims for singularity or pluralism in decision-making, or conceive of curriculum within a political context.

What, in terms of curriculum, might a 'constructive response' in the face of the loss of the stable state look like? Schon's 'constructive response' presents a number of essential features which would need to be reflected in a philosophy of Curriculum Studies that confronted the kinds of problems and issues outlined above:[37]

1 The need for public learning as a means to the solution of problems.
2 The need to move away from a dependence on rational knowledge seeking.
3 Acknowledgment of the legitimacy of the different meanings that different people attach to facts and situations.
4 Rejection of the possibility that problem solutions that are 'right' and universally applicable can be converged on.
5 Acceptance that problem situations are 'open ended' and that the search for solutions should not be closed off by adherence to fixed views on the appropriateness of ends or means.
6 Recognition of the fact that practical problems can be solved only in action.

The essays that follow look at various ways in which the adoption of principles such as these would affect our estimation of how Curriculum Studies should be thought of, and how it should go about its tasks. They suggest what kind of coherent identity it might choose for itself if it rejected those proposed for it by technocrats, bureaucrats or ideologues. The search for such an identity is not just an intellectual exercise, a private concern of those within the field. Though the curriculum decision-makers may feel that they are initiating debates the better to keep control of the curriculum in their own hands, appeals to the community are symptomatic of a major shift in the relationship between society and the school curriculum. That shift is leading to the breakdown of traditional ways of deciding what should be learned by whom and under what circumstances, and to the creation of opportunities for reconceiving the nature of curriculum tasks and the way they should be performed. What use is made of those opportunities depends on how well, as a communitiy, we learn to think about the curriculum.

2 Thinking about the practical

Curriculum tasks are practical tasks: they present us with problems we can solve only by taking action. This confronts us with a fundamental difficulty in any discussion of how and in what ways we should think about the curriculum. Thinking is associated with theorising, and theorising, it is claimed, is inappropriate to practical tasks, even inimical to their efficient performance. Theory might be useful in carrying out those curriculum tasks that can be thought of as 'proactive': where we can take an initiative, relatively free from constraint. As, for example, in the planning of a course for future implementation. But the most important curriculum tasks, those that determine what is actually realised in action, are 'reactive' in nature: an immediate, on the spot response has to be made to events that may be wholly or partly unforeseen. And these seem to escape from popularly held categories of situations in which theory can be helpful. Is this a correct assumption? Or are we inclined to overstress the importance of reactive decision-making and underestimate the extent to which we could and should interest ourselves in theorising of various kinds? Or, a third possibility, are we making a false dichotomy? Are there ways of understanding the nature of theory and of seeing curriculum tasks that avoid the necessity of being exclusively on the side of theory or practice? One easy way out of the difficulty is to separate the notion of curriculum from that of teaching or instruction.[1] We can then say that curriculum tasks – the planning and evaluating of courses – are to be seen as proactive, but that reactive skills are needed by those who have to implement and teach them. Whatever the logical or logistic reasons for making this separation, it is not likely to commend itself to us if we are interested in producing good teaching and good learning. Curricula can have an existence in the form of blueprints, but the only point of having blueprints is in order that they can be translated into action. It is in the school and the classroom that curriculum becomes a reality, and its ultimate effectiveness depends, therefore, on its being construed from the outset as something that has to be enacted. Should we then lean in the direction of saying that, since the real curriculum is the curriculum of the classroom, it is practice that matters and that theory can be relegated to a subordinate role? The activity of teaching, it can be claimed, makes the kinds of demands that have to be met by the tennis player or the footballer who has to make instant decisions on how to react. Edward Thring, a century ago, asserted that 'a man digging knee-deep, in a muddy ditch, with banks so high as to shut out the landscape, in a hot sun, and a permanent swarm of flies and gnats round his head, is no unfair description of the life of many a deserving teacher'.[2] And where is the place for theory in that situation? A further objection that is put forward, as has already been noted, is that 'theorising' is necessarily incompatible with high standards of practical performance. Teams lose, it is said, because instead of playing their 'natural' game they try to follow some theory about how to play effectively. Similarly, the argument goes, children fail to learn as well as they might because of the inappropriate and unworkable 'theories' foisted on teachers by teacher educators and curriculum experts. Though such views are often put forward as assertions without supporting argument, they nonetheless point to a genuine difficulty and demand to be taken seriously.

Of course, if we think of practice as being totally constrained by demands for instant and unreflecting action, then we may well be inclined to believe that no kind of theory has a place in decision-making: the best we can do is watch those who seem to cope well with the situation and try to emulate them. But where curriculum is concerned, we cannot allow this to be the case: we expect its processes and products to comply with criteria of worthwhileness. Teachers, if pressed, would have to deny that they are simply reacting to circumstances since to admit this would be to negate not only the teacher's autonomy, but, along with it, his status as a person engaged in an activity with moral ends. If the experience of a curriculum is to be worthwhile for students, two obligations have to be accepted by teachers. First, and most obviously, they have to be in a position to justify what is taught and how it is taught. But actions can only be justified if they are consciously chosen (pleas of *crime passionelle* enable criminals to escape punishment, not because the act was justified, but precisely because it could *not* be justified). Second, they have to be capable of modifying their behaviour in order that activities not seen as worthwhile can be avoided, and because they have to adapt themselves to changing definitions of what is worthwhile. Hence we should reject the idea that a conflict between theory and practice must arise simply because some of our actions as implementers of curricula will be of an apparently reactive nature: when we engage in curriculum tasks, we take part in an activity that has to be justified on moral grounds.[3] What we do must have some basis in ideas because they alone 'lend firmness and moral significance to action'.[4]

Yet though this general point may be conceded, the feeling of dilemma persists. Though it may be ideally desirable to assimilate the practical to the theoretical, are we not dealing with a fundamentally insoluble problem? Theory involves generalisation, but practice, it will be argued, always confronts unique people in unique situations. Every collection of teachers and students, every setting in which they meet, has its own special characteristics. As Schwab has it: 'the subject matter of the practical ... is always something concrete and particular ... this student, in that school, on the South Side of Columbus, with Principal Jones during the present mayoralty of Ed Tweed and in view of the probability of his reelection'.[5] The theoretic, on the other hand, bases itself on general statements, and how can we make general statements about the particular? Moreover, the nature of practice is determined by the personal attitudes, values and emotions of those engaged in its activities, while the theoretic is objective and rational. How can rational theory help us understand the actions of (seemingly) irrational people? Thus, even though we may allow that practice should not be merely reactive in nature, there are still reasons why a problem should exist about the relation of theory to practice where curriculum tasks are concerned.

Given this fundamental problem, it is easy to see why two antithetical traditions of thought about curriculum matters have grown up. On the one hand we have the thinking of the practitioner, fashioned through a continuing commitment to and involvement in the unique, the particular, the quirky; on the other that of the theoretician reflecting rationality, universalism and order. Action lies on the one side and knowledge on the other: intellectually and socially the two traditions fail to inform one another. 'Doing' and 'explaining' assume different priorities according to the tradition to which allegiance is given: 'The project team had to explain what it was going to do before it could do it. The teachers started by doing it and only then looked for an explanation of why they were doing it that way.'[6] But should we be so easily persuaded of the necessity of such a dichotomy? We may agree with Poincaré that 'the principles of science ... are and can only be in the indicative ... the most subtle dialectician ... will never obtain a proposition that says: do this, or do not do that',[7] but need the distinction between indicative and jussive be so closely identified with the supposed gap between theory and practice?

One way forward arises from the observation that attitudes towards theory and practice are socially determined. How we think about them relates not only to the intrinsic nature of objects and activities, but also to the ways in which we, as members of social groups, learn to value certain kinds of attitudes, behaviours and procedures. How teachers construe the functions of theory and practice depends on the roles they are called on to play in school and classroom; equally, how theoreticians feel about them is something that is conditioned by the ways in which successful theorising has become institutionalised in society. The theoretician concentrates his attention on 'reconstructed logics' – for example, idealisations of the scientific method – and neglects the 'logic-in-use'[8] of the practitioner who, consequently, grows to believe that his logic is not susceptible to theoretical analysis. Thus distinctions which owe much of their force to values promoted within social groups come to be looked on as logically valid. This is not a situation which can easily be changed, but, if we can find ways of looking at theory and practice that emphasise their similarities rather than their differences, it might be significantly modified.

Types of theory

On looking at definitions of theory, we immediately notice that much discussion of its role in relation to practice fails to make the important distinction between theory as systematic enquiry, or as the products of systematic enquiry, and theory as idealised practice. Practical activities, especially those which involve attempts to bring about improvements in human conditions, are apt to inspire theorising of the latter type. Bystanders and spectators think up ways in which the existing goals of practice could be more effectively attained, or propose alternative goals that practice might pursue. Theories produced in this way are 'inspirational'. They represent a kind of 'thought experiment' – an attempt to deduce the consequences of action without actually carrying it out. Where natural science problems are concerned, this may result in useful insights or even testable hypotheses.[9] The nature of the data and the available forms of reasoning allow this. But, in the case of the practical, the situation is different. It deals in unique contexts and uncertain outcomes ('this student, in that school, on the South Side of Columbus') so it is hardly surprising that inspirational prescriptions often turn out badly and fail to provide suitable guides to action. It is characteristic of inspirational theories that they deal in elements that cannot be defined. What exactly is an 'open classroom', or what do we mean by 'mixed ability teaching' or an 'integrated day'?[10] The fact that a prescription is inspirational is sometimes disguised because it proposes ways of handling problems that have an appearance of rationality. One well-known theory of curriculum design asserts that one should first define objectives and from there proceed to decide on the subject matter and the teaching methods that will secure those objectives. Logically, this seems an impeccable procedure: psychologically it is, in most practical situations, inappropriate. As in the case of more obviously inspirational theories, the elements do not mirror reality.[11] This is not how curricula are, for the most part, actually designed, and this is true not because of reluctance on the part of curriculum designers to improve their ways, but because of intractable features relating to the nature of the task. When so much of what is represented as 'curriculum theory' is of the 'idealised practice' type, it is hardly surprising that all theory is labelled as, at the best, irrelevant and, at the worst, misleading. It does not complement practice, it is in competition with it because it offers an idealised picture of what practice should be which usually differs from what practitioners see as realistically attainable.

Theory as systematic enquiry, on the other hand, is not normative. It does not set out to say what should be the case, though what it chooses to study should be determined by conceptions of desirable directions of development. Theory as systematic enquiry sets out to establish what is, in fact, the case and to provide perspectives for understanding how and why things work the way they do. It is naturalistic rather than idealistic. It may be objected that such theorising is essentially conservative in nature, too preoccupied with what is and too little with what might be. The reverse would appear to be the case. Idealised prescriptions put forward in ignorance of the realities of the situation provide those who oppose change with the perfect opportunity to call for a reinstatement of (an equally idealised) past, pointing to the chaos and confusion caused by poorly conceived innovations as a justification. Reform which proceeds on a secure foundation of knowledge of the nature of children, teachers, schools and classrooms has a better chance of becoming adopted into the system and affecting practice in enduring and intended ways. We do not need curriculum theories to provide us with the objectives of education. Ideas, conceptions, visions and ambitions lie all around us and it is the business of society as a whole to determine which of these shall have prior claims on our resources. The job of curriculum theory is to find ways in which conceptions can be made real[12] through increasing our understanding of the phenomena of public educational systems. From this point on, it will be theory as enquiry which will concern us.

As has already been pointed out, how we see theory in relation to practice is heavily influenced by the dominance in our society of a particular image of enquiry – that which is thought of as characterising the natural sciences. The image relates, both in the popular mind and in the minds of some theoreticians, to a highly idealised and misleading account of what scientific enquiry is and how it functions. But it is this idealised account that has been influential in the general development of theory and attitudes towards theory in those fields – especially psychology – that have been contributory to the study of education and curriculum.

> The development of the modern social sciences occurred during a period in which the science of logic was mostly concerned with the logic of the natural sciences. In a kind of monopolistic imperialism the methods of the latter were frequently declared to be the only scientific ones and the particular problems which social scientists encountered in their work were disregarded.[13]

Consequently, when the question of theory as enquiry in the field of curriculum is raised, we tend to visualise a type of theory heavily laden with 'scientific' characteristics – offering causal explanations, using precise measurement, lending itself to the repetition of experiments, to hypothesis testing, and so on[14] – a whole range of features which contrast sharply with the nature of practice as we experience it. But this is only one approach to enquiry. It is part (and a somewhat debatable part) of a wide range of concepts and techniques which make up the broad spectrum of theory as enquiry. In fact, when we examine closely the kinds of characteristics commonly attributed to scientific enquiry, we find that, far from cohering into a unique and logically compact prescription for the discovery and validation of theories, they are highly problematic in status.

While it is superficially attractive and straightforward to think of scientific enquiry as a matter of showing that event B is to be explained by the occurrence of a preceding event A, and is therefore caused by it, deeper consideration shows that no such simple conception can be logically defended. The observation that B follows A does not entitle us to say that B is caused by A, still less to infer that all instances of A will be followed by instances of B. These commonsense conclusions on the fallibility of causal explanations were reached by Hume,[15] who was led by them to extend his argument from natural events to human actions and believe that all behaviour must therefore be a matter of habit and association rather than rationality. If this were true, attempts to forge links between theory and practice would succeed by capitalising on the unfortunate conclusion that neither provided us with a context for rational action. Such a pessimistic conclusion is rejected by Popper, who accepts Hume's critique of claims that generalisations can be established from particular instances, but denies that such processes are fundamental to theorising. Theories, in his view, are not true explanations of facts, but the best approximations to truth that we can achieve, given the state of our knowledge and our critical abilities. This account of the nature of theory enables us to conceive of it as an all-embracing category with relevance to action as well as to understanding:

> not only do we reason rationally, and therefore contrary to the principle of induction, established as invalid by Hume, but ... we also act rationally: in accordance with reason rather than induction. We do not act upon repetition or 'habit', but upon the best tested of our theories which ... are the ones for which we have good rational reasons; not of course good reasons for believing them to be true, but for believing them to be the *best available* from the point of view of a search for truth or verisimilitude – the best among the competing theories, the best approximation to the truth.[16]

This line of reasoning does not imply that we are thoroughly rational creatures, but, what is important for our present purposes, it does lead to the conclusion that there is no necessary conflict between the rationality of theorising and the rationality of practical action.

The question of measurement is another consideration that has been taken as fundamental to theorising, and the result, in education, has been a vast expenditure of effort in the search for something that can be reliably measured. Unfortunately, the constructs invented for this purpose, such as IQ, have not turned out to be of great interest to practitioners, have not contributed to any advancement in our ability to justify curriculum practices, and have failed to be anything other than a conservative influence on the development of curricular goals. This practical failure has not been offset by any theoretical success: the greater the ingenuity put into measuring IQ, and the more frantic the search for other constructs to plug the conceptual gaps revealed in research programmes (creativity, N-ach), the more slippery and elusive the whole notion has become. More sophisticated measurement techniques just help to show that what it was hoped to measure was never there in the first place. But measurement, though attractive to some theoreticians and researchers, since it promises greater precision, and therefore greater scope for building and testing theories, is not essential to theorising. Even in science, the ability to make accurate measurements was a relatively late development.[17] Similarly, repeatability is not a prerequisite of physical science theorising. Many astronomical events are unrepeatable, or only repeated under changed circumstances, but this has not been an obstacle to the development of astronomical or cosmological theories, or prevented them from being accounted 'scientific'. And the role of hypothesis testing in scientific enquiry has been drastically reassessed by a number of writers who point out that, while it may play a part in attempts to disprove theories, it is far from being an essential element in their development.[18]

It can be doubted, then, whether those features of scientific theorising which have been claimed as essential to its character are really integral to it. Some, such as hypothesis testing, would seem to play a part, but not the one assigned to them by the idealised paradigm. Others seem irrelevant, or even non-existent. A reassessment of the nature and status of scientific theorising leaves the way clear for an attempt to see whether other types of rational thought or action may not, after all, share in some, at least, of the characteristics of theory making. Some writers, and notably Popper, have claimed that the similarities are, in fact, very close, while others have portrayed various types of action and enquiry as shading into one another to form a continuum with no clear boundaries. White, for example, declares that, 'philosophy has ... no clear edge to it. ... There is a gentle slope down between metaphysics or meta-ethics and practical reasoning.'[19] But to gain an idea of the extent to which various types of activity or enquiry may exhibit a common nature, it is necessary to consider separately their different aspects or stages, the grounds for instituting an action or enquiry, the processes of carrying it out, the nature of the resulting solutions and the assessment of their usefulness or truth.

Theory and practice

The grounds for taking action, whether in a practical or theoretic sense – that is, in order to deal with a situation or to understand it – lie in the perception of problems to be solved. In practice, we solve problems by taking action; in theory, by seeking for knowledge. But this is to distinguish between types of solution rather than grounds for action. When we encounter a problem, of any kind, we face a situation that is, in some sense, 'new'. As long as we are adjusted to a totally familiar environment which we have mastered we have no problems. But, as Popper suggests, 'such an adjustment is the preconscious form of developing a theory; and since any practical problem arises relative to some adjustment of this kind, practical problems are essentially imbued with theories.'[20] To accept such a proposition, one has to adopt a wide-ranging definition of theory – to allow that it can embrace any modelling of environment or means of anticipating future events whether consciously formulated (and therefore theoretic in the fullest sense) or un- or pre-conscious and implicit. But, again, it may be the gentle slope rather than the sharp cliff that faces us: formulated theories did not spring, fully armoured, into human consciousness; they evolved historically from simpler, more instinctive styles of thinking. Nor are the theories we commonly account 'scientific' always formulated in clear and unambiguous terms. An example is the theory of evolution, of which it has been said that it provides, 'not a testable scientific theory, but a metaphysical research programme – a possible framework for testable scientific theories'.[21] Recognition of the similar grounds from which explicit and implicit theories arise offers one way of dealing with the theory-practice problem. The practitioner is conscious of the existence of a problem to be solved precisely because he is confronted with events which escape his unconsciously constructed theoretical picture of the nature of his task. These constructs may include some which once figured in formal theories which are no longer recognised as such, but still influence practice. Curricula are planned, implemented and justified in ways that reflect implicit as well as explicit theories of the nature of the students for whom they are intended. A pre-theoretical notion of 'relevance', for example, is prominent in the discussion of curricula for students in the upper secondary school, and many discipline-based courses subscribe to the 'vision-based' theory of understanding, now abandoned by philosophers and psychologists, which proposes that, 'direct inspection, or intuition, results in clear ideas'. (It doesn't matter how often I *show* them, they still don't *see* it.)[22] Even modern psychological theories may reach and influence practitioners in a 'folklore' form. Piaget shapes the curriculum of younger children, not so much as a theoretical psychologist, but rather as a contributor to a stock of more or less interrelated elements that make up the implicit theories underpinning decisions to engage in curricular activities such as 'open classrooms' and 'integrated days'. (The constructs of implicit theories, it should be noted, apply generally to classes of people or events just like those of formal theories, and are not adapted to single individuals or instances.)

The grounds for theory and for practice can be seen as sharing common elements, and a similar view can be taken of theory and practice as processes. It is an exaggeration to suggest that the empirically based methodologies of science are of a highly special character and unrelated to the kinds of reasoning we would apply in other fields. All knowledge is derived from experience, if we mean knowledge of what exists, rather than knowledge of self-contained axiomatic systems, such as that of mathematics. Generally speaking, the natural scientist can draw on experience of the world that lends itself more readily to categorisation and to measurement, but the difference between data of that kind and the data that have to be handled by the practical decision-maker need not be seen as qualitative. Nor should we think of the data of science as being necessarily 'harder'. Whatever our purpose or interest, the things we observe, how we observe them and what we do with the results of our observations depend on our pre-existing theories about the phenomena in question. If scientists believe in an 'ether wind', they will expend infinite ingenuity looking for it, but if their theories do not demand that celestial bodies emit radio waves, then they will not look for them. This is a state of affairs no worse and no better than that which determines curriculum theorising where an *a priori* propensity to believe in the importance of a concept like IQ can lead to major investment in research programmes of very limited practical and theoretical consequence. 'All knowledge is theory-impregnated, including our observations.'[23] All theorists, of whatever kind, and all practitioners commit themselves to a view of the importance of certain problems and certain styles of solution, as well as to expectations that could turn out to be false and to concepts that must be taken on trust. Science may be a very sophisticated form of common sense, but it cannot transcend common sense to the extent of becoming something totally divorced from it. All thinking is committed thinking: 'Thought can live only on grounds which we adopt in the service of a reality to which we submit.'[24]

The final stage of problem solving is the proposing and evaluating of solutions. The difficulties that beset the practitioner when he has to choose or reject a particular course of action are immense. He may have addressed himself to the wrong problem, he may have answered it only in part, his solution may be mistaken or lack generality. But his discomfiture is not unique. The history of science is littered with failed theories – some of which collapsed only after initial acceptance. Geocentric cosmologies, phlogiston and caloric theories, Aristotle's theory of motion, all ranked for a while, even for centuries, as adequate attempts to solve theoretic problems, as, in the practical field, did oligarchy, slavery and the dame school. Theories, proposals and solutions of all kinds are provisional and risky. Einstein explains more than Newton, but can he cope with black holes? We cannot say that any theory or solution is the best one or the only one; we can only choose among alternatives by rational consideration of their merits.[25] Scientific theories clearly enjoy advantages in the process by which solutions are evaluated: they tend to be more precisely formulated, so that tests of worth can be more readily applied. Efficient means exist for publishing and criticising them, so that the range of available theories is well known, as are the kinds of criteria by which their adequacy should be assessed. But practical problem solvers do not inhabit a different world: they simply lack such ready means of subjecting their solutions to critical appraisal. The basic need is common to all problem solving, practical and theoretic: to establish and maintain a critical tradition within which the worthwhileness of proposals and solutions can be scrutinised. It is for this reason that ways must be found, both practical and theoretic, of drawing together the thinking styles of theorists and practitioners of curriculum. Without this, the establishment of an adequate critical tradition is an impossibility.

Provided, then, that we pay attention to the logical nature of theory and practice, rather than to the ways in which they become embedded in social customs, a good case can be made out for the 'gentle slope' model of how we respond to the problems we encounter, over the whole range from the highly theoretic to the strictly practical. In all cases some kinds of constructs determine the ways in which problems are stated; some data derived from experience are needed to enable solutions to be proposed, and some critical tradition is applied to their evaluation. Nowhere are solutions final: their success is measured by ability to move us on to new problems, rather than leave us stuck with the old ones. As Popper formalises this proposition: P_1-TT-EE-P_2.[26] That is, perception of a problem (P_1) leads us to put forward a tentative theory (or solution) (TT); this, in its turn, is subjected to a process of error elimination (or its applicability critically assessed) (EE) and, in the light of that process, we return to our problem, or to a restatement of it, or to a new problem (P_2). When modelled in this way, problem solving is seen to be a cyclical process – a notion far more recognisable to the practitioner than that of the mythical 'scientific' theory that kills the problem stone dead. We are not dealing here with qualitatively different processes, but with processes of like nature which have to be carried out under different sets of limitations. Obviously, whereabouts we find ourselves on the 'gentle slope' makes a difference. Confronted with the immediate need to find and implement a solution, we have to conduct the process of formulating proposals and eliminating error more rapidly than the theoretician who has leisure to develop and refine ideas before putting them to the test. (But, like him, we engage in these actions on the basis of a theory, though it is likely to be implicit rather than explicit.) The practical process is more likely to involve rapid iteration, a constant interaction between theory and evaluation, than to be based on carefully structured development and criticism of ideas. Our practical problems have to be answered in action, while our theoretic problems can be handled in a more reflective manner. Nevertheless, we are not confronted with an either/or choice. To ask whether teachers, administrators or curriculum planners should behave like practitioners or theorisers in solving their problems is to ask the wrong question. The choice is rather about where on the 'gentle slope' they should locate themselves, and whether they can locate themselves in such a way that all those who have to collaborate in the solution of curriculum problems can be in touch with one another within a sector delimited by the intrinsic nature of curriculum problems, the kinds of data useful in their solution and the kind of critical tradition within which the adequacy of solutions should ideally be evaluated.

50754

3 The concept of curriculum research

Adjectival qualifications of the word 'research' may have logical or heuristic justifications. The logical justifications can relate to the existence of discrete sets of phenomena to be studied, to the availability of special techniques of data gathering or analysis, to the employment of unique conceptual frameworks, or to the need to solve practical problems which exhibit common features. Thus 'cancer research' treats phenomena relating to a specific pathological condition, while 'space research' exploits a particular technology of data collection. But logical boundaries are seldom precisely delineated either in terms of the scope of a particular research field, or of its claims to uniqueness. 'Agricultural research' is concerned with solving the problems of improving yields of foodstuffs, but it also must interest itself in those phenomena which provide data for academic researchers in the biological sciences. Always, to some extent, research fields define themselves heuristically, both in the sense of their need to command public support for research activity, and in the sense of the efforts they make, as an integral part of the research process, to relocate boundaries to take account of advances in knowledge and in research technology. What I have termed 'heuristic' justifications for defining the boundaries of research fields are particularly important when matters of public policy are at issue. In these cases the research activity functions not only to solve problems, but also to define what the problems are. It matters a great deal whether we support 'road research', which implies that problems of transportation are like those of agriculture – how to get the best yield from a given surface area – or 'transport research', which takes in the wider context of movement from one place to another by any means, or 'environmental research' – how transportation can be planned as part of a complex of public amenities in competition with one another and presenting occasions for political as well as technical choices.[1] It is in these terms that justifications can be made, and definitions offered for an activity calling itself 'curriculum research'.

Taking this perspective as a point of departure preserves us from the snare of trying to make logical distinctions between curriculum research and educational research: to a large extent they can be allowed to overlap. The phenomena they study, the techniques they use to do it, the problems they concern themselves with are, to a considerable extent, common. What is distinctive about curriculum research is first that it claims to be centred on practical problems, and second that it claims to treat these problems within a set of related theoretical perspectives. There is, of course, no reason why educational research should not make the same claims: the fact is, however, that it has developed along rather different lines which, although they yield important insights into the nature of teaching and learning, seem to those who support the concept of curriculum research not to have confronted the substantive issues of how to provide the kinds of information which can lead to better decision-making on questions of what should be taught and learned. Attempts to define and support the concept of curriculum research are aimed at developing within educational research a field of activity directed towards this end. Where its boundaries lie in relation to educational research is not a particularly fruitful question: both are research enterprises which resist definition in terms of relevant sets of phenomena. What has to hold each of them together is a sense of where the central issues lie. This is a question that educational research has never made serious attempts to resolve.

Education and educational research have not, traditionally, been conceived by theorists and researchers as policy fields. Attempts to provide coherence for them have concentrated on endeavours to invest education with disciplinary status through the advocacy of particular research techniques, or through setting up criteria which would delimit the set of phenomena with which it should concern itself. Leaders in the research field, such as Kerlinger,[2] have claimed to be engaged in a process of scientific enquiry directed towards establishing lawful relationships between variables which quantitatively measure the phenomena of education. The development of curriculum research has, according to Walker,[3] been hindered by this tendency to apply a reconstructed logic of physical science research to artificial phenomena.[4] In fact, the attempt to construe educational research as a quest for natural laws and for generalisations based on the quantitative analysis of statistically chosen samples has led to fragmentation rather than coherence, as discipline-based researchers from the social sciences have turned their attention to educational data. Scheffler[5] argues that education never can be a discipline, and that we should welcome and encourage a diversity of approaches to the investigation of educational issues:

> As educators, we shall continue to ask all sorts of questions arising in the course of our work. ... We ought not to isolate ourselves from attempts to formulate [relevant principles], no matter what their

> disciplinary labels. Nor ought we to build our professional identity upon the faith that a unique discipline of education will one day be found. Rather we should encourage relevant investigations by psychologists, anthropologists, sociologists, economists, educationalists, and still others, and we should strive to link them with the concerns of schooling. There is surely enough substance in such an enterprise to support a genuine and important professional identity, indeed, several such identities. If it turns out that, in the place of a unique discipline of education, we get a variety of systematized laws and principles *applicable* ... to the practice of education, I cannot see that we will have serious cause for complaint.[6]

But this commonsense view is notable for what it leaves obscure, as well as for what it makes explicit. It does not speak of encouraging *any* investigations, but of relevant investigations, and the opening sentence suggests that relevance is to be tested by the degree to which we are helped to answer 'questions arising in the course of our work'. Later on reference is made to 'the concerns of schooling' (though without any indication of whether this is significantly different from education and, if so, how) and to 'the *practice* of education'. The underlying suggestion appears to be that practical problems can operate as a principle of coherence for education as a process of enquiry, a point made more strongly by Walker in his discussion of curriculum research: 'education, and curriculum as part of education, is defined by what it studies *and to what end*, rather than by the ideas, methods, theories or techniques it uses.'[7] But, instead of discussing *how* relevance is to be determined in terms of ends, Scheffler appears to be content to leave this vague, and to take a pessimistic view of the extent to which 'ideas, methods, theories or techniques' can be subservient to ends (this I infer from his reference to 'systematized laws and principles' which seems to imply acceptance of the view of Kerlinger and others that the only knowledge of relevance to educational questions is that which is gained by the 'methods of science'). Curriculum research, on the other hand, should be clearly related to curriculum tasks – the planning, implementing and evaluation of learning experiences – and its concern with these practical tasks will lead it to cultivate approaches other than the 'scientific' to the creation of knowledge:[8] for the kinds of knowledge required to assist in the performance of curriculum tasks are the kinds that are relevant to public policy-making. Not statements of lawful relationships which might tend to devalue the role of responsible judgment, but data that help us identify and define problems for decision and that increase our capacity for generating alternative solutions and for improving the quality of our deliberations about which of these should be adopted.

As a consequence of its colonisation by social science disciplines, educational research has never developed any coherent theory to guide programmes of enquiry, and, in view of the diversity of the phenomena it has to encompass, the absence of any overall theory is not to be wondered at. Since curriculum research is concerned with a similarly broad spectrum of data, it would be rash to claim that it could readily provide a unified and consistent set of theoretical propositions. However, there are two arguments that might lead us to suppose that curriculum research could, in this respect, provide a stronger framework than educational research for data collection and analysis. One is that concentration on tasks, rather than on the explication of phenomena, can allow us to define sub-classes of task, for which some reasonable praxiological theory might be devised. As Westbury and Steimer remind us:

> The explicit subject matter for curriculum [is] ... the potentialities that subjects, students, teachers and milieus offer, in their interaction, for an end. The end of enquiry is a knowledge of and suggestions for the variety of ways in which these potentialities *can* be actualized in terms of 'curricula' for schools and systems, course outlines, texts and materials, environmental forces, teacher models, lessons and the like.[9]

This subject matter will vary in significant ways according to factors such as the age of the student, the type and location of institution and the availability of equipment and resources. A theory that would guide us to the solution of all curriculum problems, at all times and in all places, is an impossibility. But a theory that would help us design curricula for urban elementary schools in the USA in the 1980s might not be beyond the reach of intellectual endeavour. The second argument is that, if we are concerned with task-oriented research, we do not need to look for the best possible theory, only for a theory that is adequate for the accomplishment of certain specified ends. Nor do we need a theory that is completely and consistently developed in all its parts, only one that can serve the practical purpose of directing us to helpful, task-oriented research strategies. Such theories have for a long time been available within the field of curriculum. Bobbitt's theory of curriculum design[10] was also a programme for research to guide the process of design, and in its time played a significant part in the improvement of school curricula in the USA.[11] More recent revisions and elaborations of the same basic theory, due to Tyler, Bloom and others, have had a more widespread and generally beneficial effect.[12] At the present time such theories are under attack for their inadequacies, and disillusionment with them has led some curriculum researchers to take a pessimistic view of the possibilities for developing task-oriented curriculum theories, and encouraged them to assign a purely descriptive or explanatory function to theory making. Others have applied themselves to the exploration of new paradigms that may lead towards a redirection of the style of theorising that should guide curriculum research, and have made significant advances towards showing how to generate data to assist in the design and evaluation of educational programmes.[13] Where curriculum research is concerned, it can at least be claimed that the question of theoretical bases is a live issue related to actual investigations, as is evidenced by the high proportion of books and articles on curriculum development and especially curriculum evaluation which show a concern with basic, philosophical questions of methodology. On the other hand, in educational research generally it still seems to be the case that the pursuit of particular, discipline-centred paradigms of enquiry is more important than any attempt to subsume these within a general problem-oriented theoretical framework.[14] This seemed to be the thought behind the conclusion of the Urban Education Task Force Report, *Urban School Crisis: The Problems and Solutions*, when it stated:

> While educational research has played a part in some of these projects, the general pattern has been to avoid the kind of research which deals with major learning problems. Researchers have usually singled out only limited aspects of such problems for largely financial or methodological reasons ... research with its current conceptualisation and methodology does not provide a clear sense of the broad directions to be taken.[15]

Curriculum problems and curriculum research

To a large extent, then, claims for an activity calling itself 'curriculum research' are claims for a redirection of educational research, or some part of educational research, to make it more responsive to the need to solve practical problems about designing, implementing and evaluating curricula. Coherence is given to the enterprise by its interest in problems which exhibit common features, rather than by a concern with specific sets of phenomena, or with particular techniques for collecting or analysing data. Curriculum problems are practical problems which are moral rather than technical in nature. As such they belong to a much wider class of problems. Their uniqueness lies in the contexts within which they arise, and in the kinds of knowledge required for their solution.[16] These contexts, and these sources of knowledge, are, however, not constant from place to place or time to time: it is not to be expected that any definition of the nature of curriculum problems, or systematisation of the means of treating them, can represent a 'final solution'. This is both a weakness and a strength of curriculum research. More than most other kinds of enquiry, it has to live with uncertainty, but at the same time part of its endeavours can be to show how curriculum tasks might be reconceived and redefined. It need never find itself in the position of simply providing others with the tools for the efficient realisation of policies about which it has nothing to say.

This view of curriculum research differs in some important respects from that put forward by Walker. First of all, he states the central problem which should guide investigations as, '*What should be taught, studied, and learned?*'[17] This raises two problems. First of all, while it has to be agreed that, ultimately, curriculum decisions are decisions about what *should* be done – that is, they have a strong value component – it is not the business of researchers to make such decisions. Their task, or at least one of the important components of their task, is rather, in Westbury and Steimer's formulation, to produce knowledge of the ways in which the potentialities of subjects, students, teachers and milieus *can* be actualised in terms of curricula for schools and systems. All societies provide political means whereby desirable courses of action in public education are chosen from among those that might be pursued. Often curriculum researchers play a part in making these choices, but they do so as participants in a political system, not in a research enterprise. (This raises the important question of where the researcher's commitment lies, which is taken up later.) Second, emphasis on the 'What?' question obscures the fact that in policy areas it is very difficult to separate the 'What?' from the 'How?'. Some of the discontent with earlier efforts to devise praxiologies of curriculum design arose precisely from this difficulty: what is learned is not simply a function of selection of content. The view students have of subjects in the curriculum, such as science and literature, depends on the style in which they are presented: the view they have of society or of human nature depends on how schools and classrooms are organised as much as on what is in the social studies curriculum. But the 'How?' and the 'What?' are also entangled at another level. The way in which curriculum planning itself is undertaken will affect the outcomes of the planning. The 'Naturalistic Model' which Walker[18] describes is illustrative of a planning process that is likely to have very different outcomes from that described by Tyler or Taba.[19] The one is basically political, depending on interactive considerations of means and ends, while the other is systematic, proceeding from ends to means. Given the same brief, a planning group would reach very different conclusions according to the method followed. They would also have different attitudes towards the implementation and evaluation of the courses they designed. For these reasons I prefer to conceive of curriculum problems as arising not from a question demanding as an answer a statement of content or of activities, but a question which stimulates suggestions for procedures and for the sources of data needed to enable those procedures to be effectively carried out. These procedures I label 'curriculum tasks' in recognition of the fact that the nature of the tasks cannot be exactly specified for all time, but also in recognition of the fact that, at any given time, there will be a sufficient consensus about what deserves the qualification 'curriculum', as opposed to 'administrative' or 'guidance' or 'public relations' or some other label defining part of the general enterprise of education, to enable appropriate research and theoretical activities to be undertaken.

This point, too, marks a departure from the position taken by Walker who, implicitly if not explicitly, sees curriculum research in terms of a relatively static set of tasks and techniques. Though he is critical of research which aims to identify 'isolated causes of overt behaviour in controlled situations, one variable at a time, for the purpose of verifying hypotheses not concerned with human judgments or preferences',[20] he insists nevertheless that it must be 'systematic, disciplined study of observable phenomena'.[21] It may be that these terms could be interpreted in a fairly broad way to include, for example, the approach to curriculum research used by supporters of 'illuminative evaluation',[22] but it is not entirely clear that this is so and, if it is not, how is research to be responsive to the changing frames of reference within which people arrive at judgments or preferences? The recognition that curriculum research should be problem-centred implies not only that it should embrace *some* styles of research conducive to the solution of problems, but that it should interest itself in *all* styles of research which may help in the definition and resolution of curriculum questions. These will not be exclusively empirical, systematic and disciplined in the usual connotation of these terms, nor will they be fixed. They will vary according to the prevailing context within which curriculum decisions are made, according to the mechanisms that exist for making them, and according to the aims and desires of the society on whose behalf they are made.

This observation draws attention to what is missing from the definition of the subject matter of curriculum given by Westbury and Steimer. It consists not only of 'the potentialities that subjects, students, teachers and milieus offer, in their interaction, for an end', but also of the social and political contexts within which questions of ends and means are deliberated on and the nature of the mechanisms for carrying out this deliberation. The question of how decisions on the curriculum *can* be reached is just as central to curriculum research as the question of what *can* be taught. But neither of these lines of enquiry can be pursued in a value-free way. Questions of what can be taught have an infinite number of answers: curriculum research must interest itself in a selection of such questions and in a limited range of possible answers. Limitations on lines of enquiry will be imposed to some extent by the values of society generally – what kinds of possibilities it is specially interested in – and by the values of the research community and individual researchers – what kinds of possibilities should be considered interesting in view of the theory and philosophy of curriculum studies to which they commit themselves. Questions of how decisions on curriculum can be reached are pursued in order that prescriptions can be offered for more effective decision-making. This, too, implies a commitment on the part of researchers to views on the nature of curriculum problems and appropriate means for their solution. Defining curriculum research in this way gives it a very broad scope. It implies no restriction on method, nor does it advocate that the curriculum researcher should see himself as a 'scientist' who claims to study phenomena in an academically disinterested way. It does not, however, go as far as some writers have[23] and assert that all curriculum activity is a kind of research, and that, in particular, no distinction can be made between curriculum research and curriculum development. Those who would like to abolish the distinction are free to make the attempt. If policy research defines its boundaries in largely heuristic ways then, at some point, there may be advantages in looking on research and development as aspects of a single activity. But an essential characteristic of policy fields as we know them is that they are concerned with action, with getting things done, and research is, in many respects, of an opposite nature. It is liable to ask questions which, if they were to be answered, would delay action. It is also liable to reject the premises on which calls for action are based.[24] Retaining research and development as separate concepts allows for the possibility that research and development interests can be in conflict without denying either that they will share many concerns, or that they will be, in some respects, mutually interdependent. It also saves the concept of curriculum research from becoming so diffuse that it is not clear to those who might support it exactly what they are being asked to support.

The major drawback of research programmes conceived in terms of the Bobbitt/Tyler/Taba type of paradigm is that they ignore the possibility of interaction between research designed to elicit information relevant to courses of action – data on student characteristics, social and economic needs, disciplinary knowledge and theories of learning – and research on the means by which actual judgments are made on the design and implementation of courses of action. It is only possible to decide what kinds of policy-relevant data should be sought in terms of a conception of the actual and possible means by which policy *can* be decided. Much curriculum research has, however, proceeded on the assumption that actual decision-making can conform to the curriculum theorist's view of what decision-making should ideally be like. Until recently, astonishingly little effort has been directed towards discovering how curriculum problems actually are tackled, and a disproportionate amount of this effort was devoted to the one area where the initiators of action are often themselves curriculum researchers – the summative evaluation of school programmes. This is, of course, only in a limited sense an area of action, since its function is to feed information back into the more truly action-oriented functions of design and implementation. In this respect, Walker's work on a 'naturalistic' model of curriculum development represents an important break with tradition and one which, I feel, he does not himself invest with sufficient significance in his subsequent review of the field of curriculum research.[25] Its significance lies not merely in the fact that, for practically the first time, an attempt was made to analyse and describe how curriculum decisions actually were made by a design group, but also in the fact that description and analysis had to be built on judgmental and impressionistic data and on the casting of these data into imaginative and conceptually-based theoretical frameworks. (The presentation of tables, charts and diagrams in the full case-study account obscures this only to a limited extent.)[26] More studies of this type are badly needed. A major obstacle to their production is that not all arenas of curriculum decision-making are as easily penetrated by researchers as are curriculum development projects. Agencies with a more permanent existence, such as State Boards of Education, the Department of Education and Science, Examining Boards and National Testing Services, have political reasons for allowing their procedures to remain in a certain obscurity, and the researcher cannot be assured of a ready welcome.[27] Nonetheless, a major improvement in our knowledge could be brought about if the research community and the funding agencies recognised that efforts in this direction are a prerequisite of the effective use of resources to foster research in the more traditional areas of learning and teaching. We could also then be in a position to put forward prescriptions for the conduct of decision-making with some confidence that they would be close enough to actual practice to have some influence on it.

Similarly, if we accept that curriculum decisions are always, in some sense, decisions about changing current arrangements, rather than setting up some totally new and unprecedented set of arrangements, then knowledge of current practice is always needed in order to consider what kinds of innovations might be possible or desirable. But such data are often lacking. An article in the *Times Educational Supplement* points up the problem: 'America's enthusiasm for the "new maths" is waning rapidly. All over the country there are complaints that pupils nowadays are worse at mathematics than they used to be.' So, once again, the failure to achieve basic levels of numeracy and literacy can be laid at the door of the curriculum reform movement? But wait. The article continues: 'and a survey has just found that though much was promised of the new maths, in practice it has made little difference in the schools – principally because most schools and teachers have not tried it'.[28] Which presumably means that the real culprit is the old maths? In the absence of adequate studies of schools and classrooms we cannot begin to know exactly what problems we are supposed to solve. Such studies need to be of various types. Simple 'surface' data might be produced for whole school systems – average numbers of periods devoted to particular curricular activities, results of national tests or examinations, text-books and materials in use (though publishers can be coy about releasing sales figures). More detailed investigations might be made of particular schools to monitor major curriculum variables with reference to actual programmes, teaching methods and achievement levels. But also there is a place for investigations in the tradition of what Eisner has termed 'educational connoisseurship'.[29] The activities of schools and classrooms can be appreciated and criticised in terms similar to those that might be applied to dramatic performances, and critical accounts can become inputs to judgments about the worthwhileness of curricula which bring a different (and perhaps, in some ways, more meaningful) dimension to the information available to curriculum decision-makers.[30] Research of this type is relatively expensive to carry out, and could only be attempted in a small number of sites. Clearly, its conduct depends on the acceptance on the part of the researcher of the need to take up a committed position on what kinds of curricular enactments should be valued, but, as Eisner points out, this is not the same thing as saying that his accounts will be totally subjective:

> the language used to describe educational phenomena, such as teaching, should disclose aspects of that performance that might otherwise not be seen. The critic's language is referentially adequate when its referents can be found in the work or event itself. ... An educational connoisseur should be able to perceive what the critic has described when given the opportunity to do so.[31]

The balance that needs to be struck between more generalised empirical data gathering and what Eisner terms 'thick' description[32] aimed at capturing and disclosing the culturally embedded meanings of classroom events will depend on the kinds of curriculum decision-making processes the information is intended to serve. An example of a piece of research providing a range of information from basic data to classroom criticism is Hodgetts' 1972 investigation into Canadian studies which combines some general quantification with detailed accounts of individual lessons.[33] Some national educational reports have also provided wide-ranging descriptions of existing situations, though the capture of educational research by quantitative social scientists has tended to slant their enquiries in the direction of statistical analyses of questionnaires and performance data.[34]

In order to provide information useful to those who want to move away from the *status quo*, curriculum research must look in two directions: towards information on desired states of affairs, and towards descriptions which give indications of the kinds of states that might be possible and the conditions under which they would be attainable (Westbury and Steimer's, 'potentialities that subjects, students, teachers and milieus offer, in their interaction, for an end'). Curriculum decisions are always, to some extent, political decisions. Decision-makers should, therefore, be aware of what interested parties wish to achieve, or what they would be willing to support. Not necessarily in order to reach the kinds of decisions which would be most acceptable, given people's pre-existing wants and desires. If 'deliberation' is seen as an activity integral to the effective performance of curriculum tasks, then a possible function of the activity is to act upon, as well as in response to, wants and desires. 'Every discussion of policy involves the comparison of what is or might be with some standard of what is acceptable; and it generally results not only in some action to reduce the disparity, but in some change in the standard itself.'[35] Whether or not this is true, data on the opinions of those concerned – teachers, students, administrators, voters, taxpayers and others – are needed. In this way curriculum research can provide decision-makers with the means of making judgments on how to accommodate what would ideally be liked with what can be practically achieved. This matching of ideals to norms lies at the heart of any policy-making activity, and it is principally in order that it can be carried out in education that the concept of curriculum research should be fostered. Educational research is only minimally concerned with helping us to understand what people want, and tends to deal with the possible in terms of separate factors – what children are capable of learning, what the outcomes are of various styles of teaching, the effects of grouping practices – rather than 'potentialities that subjects, students, teachers and milieus offer, in their interaction, for an end'. Interactive possibilities are ignored in favour of trying to demonstrate the superiority or inferiority of particular aspects of practice or individual characteristics taken on their own. But, while demonstration may be appropriate to the building of knowledge within an academic discipline, it is not helpful in decision-making on matters of public policy.[36] Adjudication on complex problems of matching norms and ideals requires that we attend to wholes rather than to parts and that we make balancing judgments on multiple criteria rather than decide on the basis of one piece of evidence that a course of action is to be accepted or rejected. In terms of research data, curriculum decisions will be more influenced by indications of possibilities that take account of total contexts than by attempts to demonstrate relationships between particular classroom or individual variables and particular outcomes.

This description of how research activities should relate to policy-making and decision-making on the curriculum implies that our first two curriculum tasks – curriculum planning and implementation – should not be seen as logically separate from one another. We match the norm and the ideal on the basis of a sense of what can, in fact, be changed and how that change can be brought about. If planning is not carried out in this way, it becomes a purely theoretical exercise, leading only to disappointments and frustrations. In order to have an adequate sense of how a learning environment can be changed, and what features of it we need to be able to influence in order to produce change, we need research that helps us to understand how the *status quo* came about, what tends towards its maintenance and what conflicts and dissonances point the way to possible modifications.[37] Such research has to take account of historical perspectives, of the meanings that participants place on events, of the social and political context of the curriculum and of the moral and ethical bases on which decisions about the curriculum rest. It is, in character, naturalistic, humanistic and interpretive. Though its data may be, in varying degrees, 'empirical' its treatment of data departs radically from the objectivist/reductionist paradigm in which much educational research is cast.

The third major area of curriculum tasks is that of evaluation. These are tasks concerned with establishing the relative worth of programmes of learning and teaching. What is taught and learned is the outcome of a decision-making process, so, fundamentally, when we evaluate we are asking, 'Were these good decisions or not?' To answer such a question, we should ideally scrutinise not only the activities of the school and the classroom, but also the processes of decision-making that gave rise to them. In respect of its developing orientation to evidence that can help decision-makers to make judgments about worthwhileness, evaluation is one of the healthier branches of curriculum research. The move from psychometric paradigms to concepts of 'illumination' and 'portrayal' offers the promise of sensitive and wide-ranging studies of educational practice.[38] Researchers have, however, been less ready to grasp the nettle of connecting practice with the decisions that produced it and to ask, 'Was this the right thing to do?', or, 'Was this an appropriate way to go about identifying the problem, proposing solutions and judging which one should be developed?' In 1973, the Schools Council produced a volume entitled, *Evaluation in Curriculum Development: Twelve Case Studies*.[39] Not one of these studies considered the question of whether curriculum development projects were the best means of solving the particular sets of problems that led to their establishment, nor did they enquire into the structure, management or decision-making procedures of the projects to determine whether different forms of organisation or styles of problem-solving might have led to more satisfactory curricular solutions. It is to the discredit of educational research that so little attention has been paid to this type of question. In spite of the fact that, all over the world, people individually, or more often in formal or informal groups, are reaching decisions about what should be taught and learned in schools, we have remarkably little knowledge of what connections may exist between styles of decision-making and curricular outcomes.

The future of curriculum research

Comprehensive curriculum research, designed to aid in the solution of practical problems, can flourish only if agencies of national or local government undertake a continuing commitment to it. Independent funding bodies tend to invest in fields such as education for only limited periods. On this basis they may be effective in securing advances in areas of science and social science where research traditions are already established, but they offer no real help to an activity which needs to build a tradition and can do so only over an extended period of time. The reliance of educational research on short-term injections of cash from charitable foundations, or from official agencies that offer no promise of continuing support, leads to a reinforcement of its dependence on psychology and sociology and a consequent weakening of its ability to yield data and insights relevant to practical problems about which policies and decisions need to be made. Curriculum research tends to get done when major national reports on education are commissioned – the Plowden Report was a notable example.[40] But, in the absence of support for such research as a continuing activity, the work done at widely spaced intervals for commissions suffers from the drawbacks that have already been outlined. It depends too much on discipline-centred traditions of educational research, it neglects investigation of the aims that various sections of the public hold for education, it makes too little use of descriptive techniques to improve understanding of the *status quo*, and it leaves largely out of account questions of how decisions are made and the possible constraints on their implementation. On the credit side, it can be said that, in the case of commissions, fairly direct links can exist between those who need the information and those who have to provide it. Of course, a redeveloped tradition of curriculum research would provide the members of such bodies with a better knowledge of what kinds of information might be helpful. One would anticipate that those agencies which have a continuing responsibility for the health of the school curriculum – in England the Department of Education and Science and the Schools Council – would be interested in fostering curriculum research, either in their own research departments, through bodies such as the National Foundation for Educational Research, or through colleges, polytechnics and universities. But this does not happen. In the case of the DES one can point to no instances of research being done that advances understanding of curriculum problems and how they might be solved.[41] In the case of the Council, the few contributions that have been made have stemmed largely from the initiative of outsiders and not from its own research policies.[42]

The arguments made here in favour of something calling itself curriculum research are not primarily arguments for research into completely new areas, or for the development of new research techniques. They are rather, in the terminology adopted at the outset, 'heuristic' in character. The practical curriculum tasks of planning implementation and evaluation will be carried out, in some way, whether or not we have academic writing on curriculum theory, and whether or not we have relevant traditions of research. But we can take the view that performing these tasks responsibly means that, to the best of our ability, we enquire into their nature, into the relative merits of a variety of ways of understanding them and carrying them out, and seek out those items of knowledge that will help us to act effectively in the interests of those who are the beneficiaries of the results we achieve. Research appropriate to these needs exists in only rudimentary forms, and, for reasons already rehearsed, we cannot expect that educational research as it now exists is capable of repairing the deficiency. Curriculum tasks are concerned with the reconciliation of actual and desirable states of affairs. They are also concerned with connections between intentions, enactments and outcomes.[43] Educational research tends to treat these elements as separate spheres of interest related to various contributory disciplines. The concept of curriculum research is advanced in an attempt to draw attention to the links rather than the separate elements. This implies a different attitude towards the contributory disciplines than that suggested by Scheffler. His 'variety of systematised laws and principles *applicable* ... to the practice of education' will presumably have been produced by methods seen as appropriate by individual disciplines, and their worth assessed by standards which the disciplines deem to be applicable. But what is most appropriate or valuable for the purposes of discipline-based enquiry is not necessarily what is needed for the purposes of solving practical problems. A theoretical physicist would find Newton's laws deficient in their attempts to represent the nature of the universe, but the engineer is quite happy to make use of them in order to land a man on the moon. Curriculum researchers should devise their own approaches to activities such as the formulation of theories of learning, or should at least be ready to adapt and revise the work of learning theorists to suit their own purposes. This is not to suggest that curriculum research should be free from any kind of restraint on what is to be regarded as adequate in the way of theory or evidence. Like any other kind of research, if it is to flourish it stands in need of criticism and must therefore develop standards and criteria to which criticism can be related. But these standards and criteria will relate not only to what is adequate or praiseworthy from a disciplinary point of view, but also to what is acceptable or worthwhile in the pursuit of curriculum tasks. This implies, of course, that the concept of good curriculum research is tied to a concept of what constitutes good curriculum decision-making,[44] a point which brings us back to the question touched on before of the value commitment of the researcher.

The propositions put forward here about the nature of curriculum research and about the directions in which it should develop indicate that theorists and researchers cannot adopt 'value free' positions with regard to curriculum tasks. Does this mean that they have to accept the values that others define for them? Or that certain values inhere in their professional role? Or that they are free to implement their own individual values, or respond to the values of others in whatever ways they choose? The answer is basically the second possibility, but the professional values of the researchers should be such that they feel a positive encouragement to respect and take into account a plurality of values in planning and carrying out their enquiries. A distinction was made earlier between the part played by political systems in reaching major curriculum decisions and the part played by theorists and researchers, and it was pointed out that, though the same individual might participate in decision-making in both capacities, the making of decisions was not the prerogative of the researcher in his professional capacity. The distinction is not new. It has long been fashionable for curriculum researchers to try to avoid taking up political positions by representing their role as a purely technical one. This they have done either by concentrating on questions of means rather than ends, or by representing ends as something unproblematic that can be decided without conflict of interests or ideologies. The purpose has also been served by heavy emphasis on empiricism and empirical methodologies. This stance has been criticised rightly as being, in effect, supportive of dominant values without any attempt to subject these to critical scrutiny. Those who claim that their research has practical purposes in a field where decisions have to be made on criteria of moral and ethical worthwhileness should not automatically act as supporters of the *status quo*. Neither, on the other hand, should they bring to curriculum tasks ready-made solutions whether these are technically or ideologically inspired. The position taken here is that, while the researcher can and should adopt value positions, he should do so in a professional role, and not assume that departure from a purely 'technical' stance implies that he becomes an ideologically committed decision-maker. The commitment of the researcher should be to a conception of curriculum problems as posing questions of purpose and morality at a deep level, the solution of which cannot be known in advance, but can only be discovered through wide-ranging deliberation, drawing on many sources of information including those that the researcher himself provides. Belief in task-oriented research implies belief in the possibility of improvement in directions as yet unknown, and in the ability of men to act rationally in the pursuit of such improvement.

The goal of improved decision-making can be pursued in two ways: either by raising the general level of appreciation of the nature of curriculum problems and what is needed for their solution, or by contributing knowledge and insights on specific occasions when decisions have to be made on what should be taught or learned in schools. The capacity of curriculum research for serving these purposes depends on a recognition that its processes and products are to be judged by standards and criteria suitable to a practical activity rather than an academic one. New research methodologies, or new objects of research, will do little to advance the concept of curriculum research in the absence of a willingness to adopt new perspectives for deciding how the worth of research is to be measured, but development of a concept of research that incorporates a new critical tradition can point the way towards the production of knowledge useful in formulating and solving education's central problem – what should be taught and learned in schools, and how it should be taught and learned.

4 Practical reasoning and curriculum decisions

In spite of over fifty years of curriculum theorising on the part of those who have consciously set out to develop curriculum theory, and centuries of thought devoted to wider problems of the nature of education, fundamental questions of the purposes and concepts that should characterise curriculum theory are still matters of lively contention. That this is the case is a matter of concern not only to philosophers and theoreticians, but also to all those responsible for and affected by practical decision-making on the curriculum. At a time when, all over the world, there is massive intervention on the part of governments in the shaping of school curricula, questions of how we conceptualise curriculum tasks assume a special importance: intervention is never atheoretical; it always implies some view of what the curriculum is and what theories and metaphors should guide its planning. The theory of rational curriculum design expounded by Tyler and others is, perhaps, the outstanding example of a conceptualisation that has exerted, and continues to exert, a profound and world-wide influence on the nature of curriculum decision-making.

But what do we mean by curriculum theory? We may mean a set of propositions about what the curriculum is or how it changes, but, most centrally, we mean theories about how to plan, implement and evaluate curricula. It is in order to arrive at these theories of effective practice that we interest ourselves in enquiries of a more strictly theoretic nature. Effective practice turns on effective decision-making, and decision-making in its turn is a kind of problem-solving. So we can say that curriculum theories are theories about how to solve curriculum problems. Probably few would be found to dispute this conclusion.[1] But now we come to the critical issue: what kind of a problem is a curriculum problem? Those who support planning by objectives would say that it is a procedural problem – a problem that we solve by applying a uniquely suitable formula or technique. Quite another view is put forward by Schwab who denies that curriculum problems are of such a nature that they can be solved procedurally, and argues that solutions to them must be found by an interactive consideration of means and ends. The process through which this is achieved is called 'deliberation' or 'practical reasoning'. What is proposed here is that, generally speaking, curriculum problems relate most closely to that class of questions that are referred to in some philosophical writings as 'uncertain practical questions'.[2]

We encounter uncertain practical problems as a regular part of everyday life. 'How shall I redecorate the living-room?', 'Where shall I go for my holidays this year?', 'Which party should I vote for at the next election?' But there are also questions of great public importance that have the same character. 'Should we build a third London airport, and if so, where?', 'Should Scotland and Wales have their own national assemblies?', 'Should worker directors be on the boards of all public companies and, if so, how should they be elected?' Questions of this type, whether they be everyday ones, or questions of national importance, have many features in common. First of all, they are questions that have to be answered – even if the answer is to decide to do nothing. In this they differ from academic, or theoretic, questions which do not demand an answer at any particular time, or indeed any answer at all. Second, the grounds on which decisions should be made are uncertain. Nothing can tell us infallibly whose interests should be consulted, what evidence should be taken into account, or what kinds of arguments should be given precedence. Third, in answering practical questions, we always have to take some existing state of affairs into account. We are never in a position to make a completely fresh start, free from the legacy of past history and present arrangements. Fourth, and following from this, each question is in some ways unique, belonging to a specific time and context, the particulars of which we can never exhaustively describe. Fifth, our question will certainly compel us to adjudicate between competing goals and values. We may choose a solution that maximises our satisfaction across a range of possible goals, but some will suffer at the expense of others. Sixth, we can never predict the outcome of the particular solution we choose, still less know what the outcome would have been had we made a different choice. Finally, the grounds on which we decide to answer a practical question in a particular way are not grounds that point to the desirability of the action chosen as an act in itself, but grounds that lead us to suppose that the action will result in some desirable state of affairs. The goal of our solution is not to vote for the party, but to bring about a situation where the party has power, not to give Scotland and Wales their own assemblies, but to create, through the setting up of assemblies, new political, social and economic contexts in those countries.

Uncertain practical problems, then, present many kinds of complexity. As Gauthier says, 'the sphere of the practical is necessarily the sphere of the uncertain.' A practical problem, he says, is 'a problem about what to do ... whose final solution is found only in doing something, in acting'.[3] Yet practical problems are the kinds of problems that we face most of the time and, in fact, people are quite good at solving them. It is difficult to evaluate solutions to problems that present severe uncertainty, but in conditions where solutions have to be found within known parameters, such as in games of chess, we find that the lesser computing ability of the practised player, allied to superior powers of practical reasoning, is better able than the most powerful computer to answer the question, 'What move should I play next?' or, 'What kind of overall strategy will give me the best chance of success in this position?' Where such limiting parameters do not exist, and judgments must be embedded in a wider context, one would assume that the human practical reasoner might show even greater superiority.

Practical problems and their solution

The method by which most everyday practical problems get solved has been variously called 'deliberation' or 'practical reasoning'. It is an intricate and skilled intellectual and social process whereby, individually or collectively, we identify the questions to which we must respond, establish grounds for deciding on answers, and then choose among the available solutions. But, because it is an everyday activity we tend to undervalue it and make little effort to understand it.[4] Some writers, indeed, would have us believe that the whole class of practical problems is of little interest. 'Science', it is claimed, shows us how to treat them by procedural means, and makes them easy to solve: only theoretical questions are really challenging. Of course, there are practical problems, or parts of such problems, that are not complex or uncertain and may have answers that can be reached by procedural means. If we have decided where to spend our holidays, then the practical problem of how to get to the place we have chosen may turn out to be purely procedural. We check the route maps or railway timetables and find the solution that fits our already established requirements. When we have decided to paper our living-room walls and know what kind of paper we want, appropriate calculations and measurements will tell us how much to buy. If a problem can be solved by research or calculation it can be categorised as 'procedural'. The answer to our request for help in solving it would be an indication of a known procedure to be followed, and we would make the request in some form such as, 'What must I do?' or, 'Show me what to do.' The mark of the uncertain question, on the other hand, is the question, 'What should I do?' or, 'Tell me what I ought to do.' But because this is a more difficult question, there is a strong temptation to try to reduce uncertain problems to procedural problems. Ethical prescriptions try to do this for questions of moral behaviour, books on etiquette try to do it for questions of social conduct, axiomatic philosophical systems try to do it for general questions of action and belief, and political ideologies try to do it for questions of public policy. The reduction of the uncertain to the procedural can be attempted in two ways. One is to tackle the problem at its root and to say what is important is to establish a method which, routinely applied, will provide suitable solutions. For example, to say that if we want to know where to put a third London airport we should do a cost benefit analysis. The other is to declare a goal or principle, on the assumption that if the end is agreed, the search for means is relatively simple. For example, if we agree that the end of all political action should be the establishment of the dictatorship of the proletariat, then, it might be supposed, the nature of that action will not be open to major dispute. In some respects, it could be said that the invention of principles and procedures represents progress. Culture and civilisation advance by moving things which yesterday were in the province of doubt and anxiety to the realm of the routine, leaving the mind free to turn to different and higher things. But what constitutes progress, and what represents decline in the application of principle and procedure is a matter of controversy, for both methodology and ideology may turn out to be false or misguided.

Pressures for the implementation of procedural methods of problem-solving become especially strong where the practical questions concern matters of great public concern, and large political, administrative or economic commitments may have to be made. Yet, as Gauthier points out, it is precisely in this area that we can be sure that problems do not admit of procedural solutions. He sub-divides uncertain practical problems into the prudential and the moral. Prudential reasoning, he suggests, 'may be considered to be that part of practical reasoning in which the reasons for acting are restricted to the wants, desires, needs and aims of the agent'.[5] Hence, any problem the solution of which will affect the 'wants, desires, needs and aims' of a wider population must certainly have moral aspects, and though the boundary between prudential and procedural problems may sometimes be obscure, that between moral and procedural problems is not. The attempt to deny the need for moral reasoning by setting up pre-specified objectives or procedures must fail.[6]

The preceding discussion enables us to form a hierarchy of problems. The first division of the tree is into the practical and the theoretic. The second, within the practical, is into the procedural and the uncertain, and the last, within the uncertain, is into the moral and the prudential (Figure 1). It is not claimed that every problem can be neatly slotted into one or other of these categories. In some instances, especially where the problem is vaguely felt or of a complex nature and not easily translated into specific questions, we may be unsure where to place it: in others we may face a family of problems, some of which belong in one category

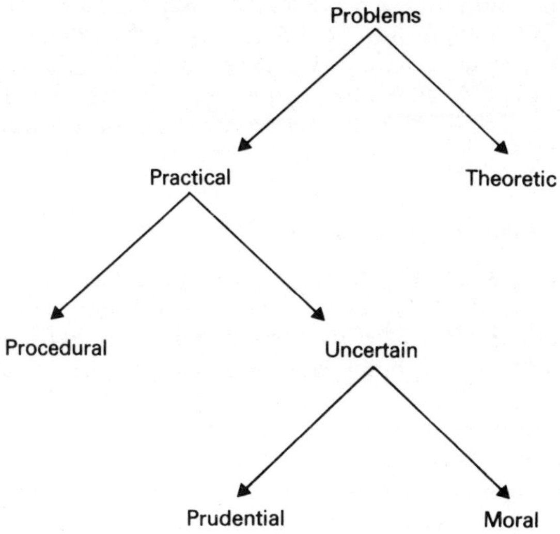

Figure 1 A hierarchy of problems

and some in another. Perhaps, even, the solution will come through shunting the problem back and forth, looking at it now in one light, now in another. The chess player may begin in procedural fashion by calculating variations according to the rules by which the pieces move. This may lead him to see how certain kinds of advantage may be secured, or disadvantage avoided. These considerations will become the grounds for a process of prudential reasoning about losses and gains which are beyond the reach of procedural analysis, or not capable of being procedurally considered in the time available. Finally, having made a provisional choice of a course of action, he may return to the procedural mode to verify that it does not contain some tactical flaw that he has so far overlooked. In this way, by appeals to different types of practical reasoning, he hopes to bring about a state of affairs which is as satisfactory as possible, given the position from which he must start.[7] However, the diagram does provide us with a useful heuristic device which will help us to decide what kind of a problem we are dealing with, and what kind or kinds of reasoning should be applied to it. It suggests that a useful guide to making this sort of decision will be a careful attempt to translate our problem into accurately phrased questions. If the question asks for a description or explanation, then it is theoretic – about knowing or understanding. 'What is being taught to thirteen-year-olds in our secondary schools?' or, 'How do young children learn?', are theoretic questions. But questions about what to do, or how to do it, are practical. If they ask for suggestions about method, they are procedural: 'What must I do?' If they ask for adjudication about preferences as well as about procedures, they are prudential: 'What should I do?' If they require the use of words like 'ought', then this adjudication has to take account of moral and ethical as well as prudential considerations. The last distinction is difficult to make: when we use words like should and ought, it is not always clear whether we are asking prudential questions or moral ones.[8]

The nature of curriculum problems

This discussion of the nature of practical problems clears the way for a closer consideration of the central issue to which curriculum theorists and practical educators need to address themselves: what kind of a problem is a curriculum problem? Curriculum problems inhere in the practical concerns of a particular task area. The task set consists in the solution of a primary set of questions about *what* students should learn, and also in the solution of a secondary set of questions about *how* decisions on desirable learning programmes should be taken and implemented. Our conclusions about what kinds of questions these are will determine our views on what kind of theoretical stance we should adopt when we attempt to solve them. A consideration of curriculum problems suggests that they have all the characteristics of uncertain problems. First, they pose questions that have to be answered. Second, the grounds on which we have to make decisions are unsure. We can see that if someone says, 'But why do you teach that?' he is not asking for a formal proof that what we are doing is what *must* be done, but a justification, a reasoned argument to show that what we are doing is the outcome of a rational consideration of a range of possibilities. In practice, of course, the questioner may get a different type of response, one which disclaims responsibility and points to constraints that preclude choice. However, our concern here is with the expectations within which the question is framed, rather than with the range of possible answers. These will be considered later. Third, we already teach something and that something is a necessary point of departure for any fresh process of decision-making. Existing resources, expertise and expectations have to be taken into account. Fourth, we have to make our decisions relative to a unique context. Fifth, we have a problem about conflicting aims and how to adjudicate between them. We may want our students to enjoy themselves, but not so much that they forget what they are supposed to be learning: to obey instructions, but also to think for themselves: to work quickly, but also to be accurate. Sixth, we know that, whatever we decide to do, the outcome will be, to a degree, unpredictable. Finally, the justification of an act of teaching lies not in the act itself, but in the desired ends we intend to achieve by it. This characterisation of the nature of decisions about teaching is put forward as self-evident and unproblematic because it is likely that teachers would agree with it. But perhaps this agreement would be based on a limited and partial view of what such decisions entail? And why, in any case, should we suppose that the question of what to teach is all pervading in curriculum decision-making? Is this not to oversimplify or even to preempt the question of the nature of curriculum tasks? Evaluation, certainly, implementation, possibly, and perhaps even design could be seen as essentially procedural matters. Indeed, they traditionally have been seen as procedural matters by curriculum theorists. Tyler's rationale for curriculum planning clearly points the way to a concept of curriculum design based on procedural principles. It can be argued that this is not how Tyler himself saw it, and that his concern was more to show how some parts of the deliberative process could be brought within procedural rules.[9] However, theorists of a more technological bent have developed 'rational' curriculum planning to the point where the deliberative elements are relegated to insignificance, so that agreement on ends is treated as totally unproblematic and is separated off from agreement on means which is to be arrived at through the application of a sequence of predetermined moves.

As I suggested earlier, there always will be those who think, for one reason or another, that the ends of education are fixed, whether these be the teaching of so-called 'basic skills', initiation into existing modes of social behaviour, or preparation for some utopian state of affairs that is just round the corner. Study of curriculum practice, however, suggests that ends are never fixed, and that this is not due to some temporary difficulties that will be cleared up when we have more knowledge, more resources, or better means of enforcing an officially approved ideology. Even in totalitarian states there can be sharp disagreements about which proximate ends are in tune with ultimate ideals, and, still more, controversies over which means are implied by the chosen ends. Does one, for example, best induce conformity by repressive authoritarianism – the imposition of values – or by forcing people to seek their own sources of social stability through group processes – Rèisman's 'other directed' man?[10] But even if values are in dispute, should there not be, at least in the realm of major decision-making on the curriculum, the possibility of applying some kind of 'scientific' procedure to problem solution? At this level, the pressures are great to arrive at effective and efficient decisions and there is also the opportunity of developing special expertise which could not be available to every teacher in every classroom, or even to every curriculum developer in every curriculum project. The analogy might be between the householder deciding where to put his garden shed, and the Government where to put the third London airport. In the second instance a huge investment of money is at stake, and there are vast implications for housing, for industrial development, and for the creation of ancillary transport services. Surely the expert who can offer a method, a procedure, will pay for his keep, however expensive that turns out to be? The Roskill Commission on the Siting of the Third London Airport undertook the most thoroughgoing cost benefit analysis ever to be attempted in England. The Commission's enquiry was hailed as 'the most rational, dispassionate procedure that good minds could devise'. Allied to the expertise of the cost benefit analyst was the experience in weighing evidence of a High Court judge. When the Report appeared it immediately aroused such a wave of protest that its recommendations for an inland site were set aside in favour of a decision to develop the Foulness site which the Commission had ruled out at a very early stage in its proceedings, and had only considered in its Report, in order to reject it, because of insistence that one maritime location should be included for comparative purposes.[11] The lesson of Roskill is that public decisions affecting large numbers of people in such a way as to influence the nature of the lives they lead must be moral and political decisions. A rational model of enquiry assumes some limited and predetermined view of human wants and desires, but wants and desires are always various and contradictory. As McKeon suggests, logistic solutions of practical problems 'stand in need to a science of human action to guide the uses of the sciences', because 'when it is proposed to apply science to practical problems, the conception of the practical is determined by the conception of scientific method which is employed'.[12] Landing a man on the moon is a practical problem to which, once the project has general approval, scientific procedures can and should be applied, both in producing the necessary hardware and in setting up the social systems to operate it. Those immediately involved can be fitted into the technology, while the remoter public participate only as taxpayers – a simple role that can be encompassed by a simple theory of human nature. But in cases where decisions have to be taken that intimately affect the ways of living of whole communities it seems highly unlikely that any scientific approach could be found that would reflect such a complex and varied conception of human nature that the procedure could cater for all wants and all values. The distinction, as Daniel Bell has it, is between 'games against nature' and 'games between people'.[13] But what of the objection that in any case too much prominence is being given to the question, 'What should be taught?'

It is true that many curriculum problems and tasks are subordinate ones that do not involve us in asking fundamental questions about what should be taught. Nevertheless, when translated into the question form, they present us with decision situations to which the same kinds of characteristics apply. If we are asked to evaluate a curriculum, 'What should I do?' is a more appropriate way to request help than, 'What must I do?' – and this is not simply because we have not yet found the time or the ingenuity to devise the method that must be employed because it is the right one. The answer must be, 'It all depends – on the context, on the ends in view, on who wants the evaluation and for what purpose.' If we agree with Hampshire that 'there is no means of establishing a *universal* connection between a specified action, and the reasons for and against performing it, in virtue of which certain reasons *must* be accepted as good reasons independently of everything else',[14] then the evaluation procedure must always be contingent. Our practical reasoning about it will lead us to prefer one procedure or set of procedures to another, and at that point our style of reasoning will shift to the logistic mode. But an immediate decision to apply a given technology imposes a solution dictated by logistics rather than by the situation to which it is applied, and runs the risk of sponsoring an irrelevant action.

To sum up the argument: it is claimed (1) that problems can be divided into two basic categories of theoretic and practical, and that curriculum problems can be seen as falling within the sphere of the practical. (This is not, of course, to say that answers to theoretic questions are not needed for the solution of curriculum problems; only that the practical sets the context within which such questions are raised.) (2) That there are various ways in which practical problems can be solved, depending on the extent to which they must be regarded as 'uncertain' on the one hand, or 'procedural' on the other. (3) That problems are uncertain when the grounds for decision are unclear, when there are conflicts of aims, when the problems relate to unique contexts, when other people with varying wants and desires are affected by the solutions to them – any one or more of these features points to the existence of an uncertain problem. (4) That curriculum problems present all of these features, first because they relate to a fundamental question, 'What should we teach?' that exhibits them, and second because curriculum tasks, though they may be suited to some kinds of procedural treatments, are embedded in unique contexts that must be deliberatively appraised before these solutions can be chosen. The conclusion is that the main instrument for the solution of curriculum problems must be deliberation, or practical reasoning.

Is this the same thing as saying that, on the whole, logistic methods are inapplicable to curriculum problems and that, as a result, we should leave the practitioners to find solutions by whatever means common sense would seem to dictate? This would be a totally wrong conclusion. Practical reasoning is not the same thing as common sense, though it may owe a great deal to it, as do all kinds of reasoning.[15] First of all, conceptions of the practical, though they do not treat of theoretical questions, are not on that account to be regarded as in themselves untheoretic. As McKeon points out, 'the expression of practical philosophies depends, despite their quest for concrete foundations, on the formulation of a theory which takes its place among other theories'.[16] Second, the skills of the practical rest on the identification and refinement of a stock of knowledge that is the result of artful practice and contemplation. To return to our analogy with playing chess, the superiority of some players over others is not just a matter of ability to act procedurally in analysing lines of play, but of applying practical reasoning to the evaluation of positions.[17] It is clear that these practical reasoning processes have been improved over a long time span by generations of expert players, and that they can be described and taught. A tradition of practical reasoning is built up through extending, elaborating and refining the criteria by which actions are to be justified, and showing how these criteria are to be weighed in practical situations. The growth of the tradition is made possible by the collation and discussion of examples of practice, by the insights of gifted individuals and the discovery of new possibilities through experimentation. The result is a formal and accessible body of knowledge, not of a commonsense nature, about how to engage in effective deliberation.

Curriculum tasks: Research and analysis

Returning to curriculum tasks, we can equally well suppose that ways can be found of improving powers of practical reasoning to aid in their performance and, in this instance, of creating contexts in which they can best be deployed by people working both individually and in groups. That this has not occurred, or has occurred only to a limited extent in curriculum decision-making, can be attributed to a number of facts – that performance is not easy to evaluate, that practice is less visible (in some areas hardly visible at all), and that experimentation has tended to be conducted on the assumption that what is needed is not a way of treating curriculum problems as practical problems but of reducing them to procedural ones.

Some work has, however, been done specifically in the area of curriculum decision-making that helps us to see how notions of practical reasoning can be applied to it. Scheffler, in his article 'Justifying curriculum decisions', characterises curriculum decisions as 'controllable acts', what he calls 'moves'.[18] Moves, he says, imply responsibility, so that justifications for them must be based on practical reasoning, not on rational or scientific deduction, for that would mean that we could somehow prove that what we had done was logically inevitable – 'we consider decisions on educational content to be responsible or justifiable acts with public significance'.[19] In such situations, many things are justifiable, but some are more justifiable than others. It does not follow, however, that we are never able to deny responsibility for our acts. We might be able to claim that we were constrained totally by forces we could not control. 'I teach it because it is in the official curriculum, which I am legally obliged to implement.' An important consideration here is the legal and administrative framework in which curriculum decisions have to be taken. A curriculum decision in Sweden, where the curriculum is an Act of Parliament, is not the same as a curriculum decision in England, where content is a matter for negotiation within more loosely formulated sets of constraints. The question of the role played by the individual within the system is also significant. Disclaimers of responsibility might be acceptable from teachers, but we would be less happy if those who play a part in the constraining context were to justify themselves in this way – state boards of education, examining board syllabus panels, or directors of curriculum projects. At some point we would always feel obliged to demand an explanation based on practical reasoning. This could take the form of a 'relative' justification – one which showed that the decision fitted in with generally accepted facts, policies or preferences. This is reminiscent of legal justification – showing that a particular act is to be regarded as a member of a special sub-set of acts – burglary or arson; or perhaps to be excluded from it – not acting *in loco parentis.* But sometimes even this form of explanation would not content us, and we would demand not a 'relative', but a 'general' justification. Here the scope of practical reasoning would be expanded to its fullest extent. Evidence in the form of theories or data might be cited, discussion of fundamental purposes embarked on, notions of the nature of man and of education elaborated.

Scheffler, then, gives us ways of thinking about how, and to what extent, practical reasoning may enter into curriculum decisions by distinguishing three levels of justification: the forced move (which might be referred to as a 'non-move' since it is totally constrained), the move having 'relative' justification and the move having 'general' justification. These can be compared to the three types of question previously discussed: questions of what 'must' be done, what 'should' be done and what 'ought' to be done. His analysis also suggests that the levels can, to some extent, be equated with levels of organisation, and that, therefore, people operating at these various levels will have different attitudes towards the nature of the processes that should guide curriculum tasks. Classroom teachers will feel themselves to be the most constrained and will be the least interested in theory and data, because they are not called on to justify their actions in general terms. Administrators will be concerned with relative justification – accepting policy frames and determining what actions fit those frames, while those responsible for producing ideas and innovations will have the greatest concern with the appeals to theory and data that general justification implies. This dispersal of the focus of argument and justification is exemplified in studies of curriculum innovation such as Shipman's *Inside a Curriculum Project*, or Smith and Keith's *Anatomy of Educational Innovation.*[20] This situation is not likely to change dramatically. True, there is some movement in schools towards more open styles of learning which would demand more appeals to general justification – situations in which the possibilities for action are multiplied stand in greater need of this than those in which action is largely predetermined.[21] Also, it is the case that some countries have to adapt themselves to major reorganisations in the educational system. In such cases, we can expect an increased interest on the part of teachers in ways of generally justifying their curriculum decisions. But the sheer size of the educational enterprise makes it certain that a large part of curriculum decision-making will always be, in one way or another, routinised. Otherwise the decision-making capacities of the system will be overloaded. Protests about 'too much innovation' are protests about the strain of having to justify things. We may in fact expect that in England many schools and teachers will welcome increased national control over the form of the curriculum, since this removes part of this particular burden from them at a time when the scope they have for exploring new possibilities is in any case limited by declining student populations and scarcity of resources.

Scheffler's analysis helps us to see how various modes of practical reasoning might be related to a variety of curriculum tasks. A closer examination of how practical reasoning might be applied to a more specific kind of decision-making situation is offered by Schwab in his article 'The practical 3: translation into curriculum'.[22] His main concern is with processes of deliberation in small groups gathered together to design curricula. The point of departure of his argument is that group deliberation is essential to the kind of decision-making that is required when curriculum design is to be undertaken, because only the group can gather together all the kinds of evidence and expertise that are needed and make them available to the judgmental process. The intention of his paper is to suggest what the nature of curriculum design as a task demands in the way of processes of group deliberation. He distinguishes five sources of expertise that are needed in curriculum deliberation, and three kinds of process that must be engaged in. The sources of expertise are: discipline(s), learners, milieus, teachers and curriculum making. The processes are: discovery, coalescence and utilisation. He suggests that the group should consist of ten or twelve people, so that the sources of expertise can all be well represented without creating a group so big that it is too formal. Informality is important because, without it, discovery of relevant knowledge is made difficult. People are afraid to risk assertions or, on the other hand, to contest them. Their concern may be more with defending positions than discovering wants, aims and possibilities. This emphasis on discovery echoes the views of both Hampshire and Gauthier on the nature of deliberation. 'Coming to know what one wants is partly a decision and partly a discovery', and 'Only as we consider what we can do or not do, can we determine what wants and desires, aims and ends, may be effected by our action. As a result of this enquiry we establish practical judgments.'[23] Discovery of other people and their wants and desires leads to an amalgamation or coalescence of aims, data and judgments. The knowledge and awareness thus created must then be creatively used to produce a curriculum design. But Schwab sees these processes as alternating rather than sequential: 'The process is carried forward in a spiral movement toward a body of generated educational alternatives and choices among them.' Also, he considers the process to be intrinsically educative. Good decisions will be made because they will be taken in view of an exhaustive and honest appraisal of needs, possibilities and criteria for choice. However, he realises that this is an ideal that curriculum groups often fail to achieve. Most often, he considers, this is because discussion is dominated by scholars – disciplinary experts – who present subject matter as a model rather than a source, preempting many possible solutions. Equally bad, however, is the opposite problem which arises when the problem is construed as, 'How can we use science (etc.) to achieve x, y or z? Where the x, y or z originate the deliberation and the scholarly materials are dragged in by the heels.'[24] These are all aspects of a wider problem that he expresses as follows: 'It is "normal" for men to treat their own values as if they were well examined, to ignore contrary or different values utilized by others, and, most of all, to elevate automatically the area of their own expertise to the role of ultimate arbiter of matters under consideration.'[25]

The techniques suggested for improving deliberation usually involve considerable expenditures of time. Schwab, for example, thinks that as many as ten meetings may be needed to establish a basis for taking curriculum decisions. He further suggests that the curriculum specialist should function in the group as a 'countervailing force'. Presumably, though he does not say so, Schwab sees the curriculum specialist as the person who should chair the discussion, on the grounds that he is, more than any of the others, a disinterested party able to guide the process of mutual discovery. The curriculum specialist, on this view, would be more a person skilled in managing groups than someone with factual knowledge of curriculum construction. The lack of further, more specific suggestions stems, as I have suggested, more from the fact that the attention of theorists has been focussed on the elaboration of logistic procedures than from the fact that such suggestions are hard to discover, and, in response to Schwab's lead, they are now beginning to come forward.[26]

Deliberation in its purest form is likely to be found in situations where there is consciousness of the need to justify decisions in general terms, and where group members are in sufficiently prolonged contact to be able to engage in the discovery process. Such conditions are encountered in curriculum project teams. Several studies have been made in project groups, the most detailed being that carried out by Walker.[27] His curiosity was aroused by the fact that groups in which he had participated had never operated on the procedural basis advocated by the exponents of rational theories of curriculum planning.

> I had come West [he says] to study education in hopes of learning how curricula should be developed. I had seen what seemed to me to be an inordinate amount of fumbling around, false starts, uncoordinated effort, misunderstandings of purpose, failures to sustain an agreed-upon directness across long units of work and just plain mistakes of conception and execution. I thought there must be a body of lore somewhere that would enable curriculum makers to profit from the insights and mistakes of their predecessors. Surely others with more experience who have been able to give the problem more thought would have written of these things? But when I began to read in curriculum I found advice that seemed appropriate to another activity altogether. 'First state your objectives'.[28]

So he set out to find an answer to a theoretic question which might help to solve his practical problem. To see how curricula should be planned, he tried to discover how they are in fact planned. How do design teams arrive at a common understanding of the purpose and direction of their work? How do they organise their tasks? How do they use their understanding of the purpose and direction of the work to produce plans and materials? To do this he made a case study of an art project at Stanford University directed by Elliot Eisner. He listened to discussions and made and analysed tape-recordings of them. At first the talk seemed random and ill-directed. But the more he studied it, the more functional and purposeful it began to appear. Drawing on a number of writers, including Gauthier and Toulmin, he devised a scheme for analysing the discussions of the project group. First he located what he called 'episodes' – sequences which were given a unity through the treatment of some single theme in a uniform style of discourse. Then, within the episodes, he tried to find a finer structure. This led him to propose six kinds of deliberative move: proposals, arguments (for and against), clarifications, instances and a miscellaneous 'other' category. The terms are self-explanatory. Proposals for action are put forward (though they may be implicit rather than explicit in what is said). Points are made for and against such proposals. Attempts are made to clarify a point, to clear up misunderstandings about it, and instances are quoted to illustrate what is being conveyed through proposals or arguments. Walker found that observers could be trained to produce analyses along these lines with a good degree of reliability. He then went a stage further, and asked about the actual content of the deliberative moves. What kinds of data did they draw on and what were the data about?

His work establishes two main points. First that curriculum deliberation as it is customarily practised is not random. It is structured and task relevant. This suggests that it can be studied with a view to establishing principles and methods for raising the capacity of groups for effective problem solving.[29] Second, that it is possible to characterise the nature of any given piece of deliberation in terms of the data on which it draws. Thus we can evaluate it by studying how effectively data were used to state problems, to define the area within which solutions could be sought and to justify the arguments and judgments that guided choice between possible solutions.

Walker's conclusions did not cast doubt on the intrinsic value of the deliberation process, but they did show that the data base on which it proceeded was rather slight. He found that rather more than half the arguments he analysed were based on experience, conventional wisdom or speculation rather than observation; that, where observations were quoted, about half were made within the project rather than outside it; that most of the observations quoted had been made personally by team members and did not result from a search for research evidence, and that, of these observations, the majority were made incidentally and not purposefully. In terms of Schwab's categories, there was fairly frequent reference to disciplines and learners, but other categories, and especially data from areas beyond the school and the classroom, tended to be ignored. Walker comments:

> there is [an] almost complete absence of talk about society, about the world outside the school. Traditionally this source of information has been regarded, along with the student and the subject matter, as one of the three factors that should always be considered in developing a curriculum. Some writers have gone so far as to subsume the others under this one, since many characteristics of students and presumably all characteristics of subject matter are socially determined. Yet virtually none of the arguments in this sample of the deliberations of three projects appealed to data about the society.[30]

National decision-making on the curriculum

Curriculum decisions, other than those of a very trivial kind, are, in the words of Scheffler already quoted, 'responsible or justifiable acts with public significance'. In extreme cases, such as decision-making on curriculum structure and content at the national level, we may wonder to what extent analyses such as that of Gauthier, which is based mainly on personal decision-making, are capable of revealing the nature of the problem-solving process. In fact, though they may have some unique features, curriculum questions at a high policy level seem not to be intrinsically different, in important aspects, from questions of the type suggested earlier in this discussion: 'Should we build a third London airport and, if so, where?' 'Should Scotland and Wales have their own national assemblies?' 'Should trade unions appoint directors to the boards of public companies?' We can recognise in these those kinds of practical problems which, in Scheffler's terms, require solutions having a 'general' justification, and which Gauthier would classify as 'uncertain'.

Attempts will be made to treat them as procedural – as in the case of the Roskill Commission – or as questions requiring only relative justification – strong public challenge was required to gain acceptance of the principle that the need for new motorways in England should be demonstrated on general grounds, and not simply in relation to Department of the Environment projections on traffic flow which, though suspect, *had* to be accepted.[31] But we feel, rightly, that only some of the factors involved in such decisions can be subordinated to a predetermined procedural treatment, and that, though major decisions of public significance should be justifiable in terms of general policies, the nature of this justification should be unique to the particular decision. We are not happy that the cost benefit analyst should do his sums and prove that the new airport should be put at the bottom of our garden, or that the constraints of policy should dictate that a motorway should be built through a national park.

How we in fact deal with practical questions at the national level and how we should deal with them is the theme of Vickers' book *The Art of Judgment*.[32] The analysis given of the process of decision-making suited to the solution of national policy questions closely parallels that suggested at a different level by Schwab. Five stages of decision-making are defined though, as in the case of Schwab's stages, they are not necessarily sequential. The stages are: appreciation – how the problem is to be defined; reality judgment – what the relevant facts are; value judgment – what solutions would be acceptable; generation of alternatives – what might be done; and proposals – what should be done.

The concept of appreciation relates to the fact that important questions of policy do not present themselves in clear and unambiguous terms. We start from a feeling that a problem exists and that action should be taken to solve it. We probably also have some notion of what the problem might be about and how it could be framed in terms of specific questions. But, if we rush too quickly to an assumption that the problem has been adequately stated, we may waste time and resources on trying to answer the wrong problem, or a problem which it is not within our capacity to treat, or can only be treated at great expense. Vickers quotes the example of problems about traffic in towns. In England in the early 1960s this tended to be construed as a problem of how to enable city roads to carry heavier traffic loads. The Buchanan Report of 1963 came to quite a different conclusion. It construed the problem not as one of road development, but of traffic regulation, and it drew attention to the fact that even this problem could not be solved unless it was seen as part of a wider problem, 'of relating the needs of transport in and through an area with the needs of life within that area; and this is a problem of town planning in three dimensions'.[33] Finding out what the problem is entails the participation of a variety of people having a range of expertise and viewpoints. This conclusion parallels Schwab's point about sources of expertise. At the national level, royal commissions are examples of bodies appointed not necessarily to recommend action, but to 'appreciate' a situation. They expose what they regard as the relevant facts, make clear their value judgments on these facts and describe the processes by which they have connected facts and values in order to reach conclusions. Thus they provide the authority that appointed them, and also anyone who reads their report, with a common basis for forming their own appreciation. Vickers sees appreciation as a two-way process. Facts and opinions interact. Appreciation is educative in the way that deliberation is seen by Schwab as generally educative. People's minds are changed by the act of appreciation. They come to see things in new ways and therefore to change their views on what constitutes the facts relevant to judgment. Since appreciation is educative, it is a worthwhile activity in its own right, even if recommendations for action are ignored. Commenting on the Gowers Report of 1953 on capital punishment, Vickers observes:

> if all the recommendations for action had been ignored, the major importance of the report as an appreciative judgment would have remained the same. The state of the commissioners' minds on the subject of capital punishment, after they had made this appreciation, was different from what it was when they began; and this change, communicated through the report, provoked change, similar or dissimilar, in greater or less degree, in all it reached, from serious students to casual readers of newspaper paragraphs; and this released into the stream of events and into the stream of ideas an addition to the countless forces by which both are moulded.[34]

If he is right, then the time spent on such activities is to be seen as an investment and not just a cost.

The next two categories both contain the key word 'judgment'. However thorough and educative our appreciation of a situation, what we eventually do is a matter of judgment – judgment about what knowledge is of relevance to a decision (reality judgment), and judgment about what courses of action might be possible (value judgment). Judgment is the companion of justification and therefore of responsibility. 'Judgment', says Vickers, 'is an ultimate category, which can only be approved or condemned by a further exercise of the same ability.'[35] In legal affairs this is plainly true; a lower court gives a judgment, a higher court confirms or reverses it.[36] But these are both judgments; we do not know that one is better than the other, only that one is more authoritative than the other. In all situations where we must face practical problems of an uncertain nature we have to make judgments and be held responsible for them. We cannot escape by saying that, because we adopted an approved method, formula or procedure, what we did must have been right. Reality judgments are made difficult by the fact that what is the case may be a matter of dispute and by the difficulty of deciding what, in the light of our appreciation of the problem, constitutes relevant information among the facts and opinions advanced by various interested parties. Where part of the reality judgment concerns what people feel, value or believe, then the problems of exercising judgment are magnified. The making of reality judgments is, therefore, 'a critical and an integrating mental activity',[37] not just a matter of routine fact gathering. Value judgments connect facts to possible actions by examining the benefits they might bring or the disadvantages they might entail, so that their acceptability can be assessed. Some actions might be excluded on moral grounds, some because of the unwanted side effects they might provoke, and some because they might be expensive or ineffective. Value judgment on possible actions lays the ground for making sets of alternative proposals that can be compared and evaluated. From these will emerge a final set of proposals – a plan for action. But the categories may interact with one another: the realisation of the implications of a particular possibility for action may lead us to re-examine our appreciation of the problem, or an insight in the reality judgment phase may directly suggest a definite plan of action.

Vickers does not deal in any detail with the composition of deliberative bodies on major national issues, but his analysis of procedure would lead us to suppose that his recommendations would not be very different from those offered by Schwab. Large groups will find it difficult to engage in an honest and open interchange of ideas; people who represent 'constituencies' may impair deliberation by acting in a political way; exclusion of important sources of data and opinion will lead to faulty judgments. (McKie quotes the case of an inter-departmental committee on the third London airport that sat from 1961 to 1963, and which demonstrated the classic dangers in staffing a committee. Of its fifteen members, thirteen were from aviation.[38]) A further problem in the case of committees and commissions is that of deciding on the terms of reference. Vickers' concept of the process of appreciation demands that there should be a very broad freedom to define the nature of the problem to be answered. Yet the terms of reference often do not allow for this (the various airport commissions were not permitted to suggest that growth of air traffic should not be allowed, or that it should be catered for in some other way than by building a third airport in the south-east of England). We might deduce also that the personal qualities demanded of those who participate in the processes described by Vickers will be much the same as those required of members of Schwab's deliberative groups.

Implications for the practice and theory of curriculum

If we accept that decision-making on the curriculum at all levels is a matter of solving uncertain practical problems, and that the kind of reasoning required is of the type described by writers such as Gauthier, Schwab, Scheffler, Walker and Vickers, what conclusions should we draw? First of all there are implications for curriculum theory. With a few exceptions, some of which have already been discussed, curriculum theorists have assumed that the character of its problems is such that their solution lies in the discovery of logistic procedures that provide a rational method for deciding on content. If curriculum problems are seen rather as being principally amenable to practical reasoning, to which method and procedure must be subordinate, then a number of deficiencies in the current state of curriculum theory become apparent. It has failed to provide us with understandings of the nature of deliberation and especially of the ways in which curriculum deliberation may exhibit unique features not shared by other forms of deliberation. By concentrating on method it has neglected to show how method is to be translated into practice through human agency or social system, and through concentrating on selection of content it has overlooked the fact that what is designed must be governed by understandings of the milieus within which it is to be enacted. Design theory has grown up in isolation from implementation theory which is an essential input to all stages of deliberation.[39] An overcommitment to the rationalist approach has encouraged a futile search for *the* theory of the curriculum, when an understanding of the nature of deliberation suggests that there must be multiple theories for multiple contexts. It has encouraged an erroneous belief that curriculum theory can, in some way, point to a 'value free' method of reaching curriculum decisions, whereas it is of the essence of the deliberative approach that values are central to decision-making, and not to be denied. It suggests the possibility of final solutions when, in fact, changing situations constantly raise new problems and call for new appraisals. Deliberative problem-solving is called for precisely when the process is a cyclical one, leading from old problems to new ones. Finally, by adopting a narrow frame of reference for the statement of curriculum problems, it has drawn attention away from the need for careful appreciation, in the sense in which Vickers uses the word, and presented problems as reducible to questions of appropriate objectives, content and methods. The deliberative approach demands that we test such assumptions, and enquire whether curriculum problems may not sometimes be problems of administration, or personal relationships, of ideologies, of community life or of democratic participation.

If we accept the arguments in favour of seeing curriculum problem-solving as an exercise in practical reasoning, then there are consequences both for the conduct of curriculum tasks and for the skills demanded of those who undertake them. The two are essentially interdependent. Unless there is a belief that it is possible for decision-makers to act other than as representatives of constituencies of one kind or another, unless there is confidence that time spent in exploratory and appreciative discussion is well invested, unless it is accepted that better data lead to better decisions, then the opportunity for people to gain the skills of deliberation will not exist. The unfortunate truth is that, over a long period of time, these skills have been declining. This is true in fields other than that of curriculum decision-making; in many areas of public policy expediency, procedure, majority votes and authoritative pronouncements have gradually usurped the place of appreciation, deliberation and judgment. Generally, this can be attributed to the increasing rate of decision-making that has to be sustained. Specifically, it has resulted from a desire to achieve greater 'efficiency' by seeing ends as unproblematic and using 'science' to solve problems through the application of increasingly sophisticated means. Scientific management, cost benefit analysis and management by objectives are all, within certain limited spheres of application, useful techniques for problem-solving; all have, in their time, been stretched far beyond their range of convenience in the belief that they can save us from having to adjudicate between competing and incompatible goals, and have led us into situations where problems get treated not because they are the problems that matter, but because they are the problems for which some procedural technique exists. At the same time, the social systems on which decisions have to be made have become more complex, bureaucratised and routinised. The purposes for which they exist tend to become lost under the administrative apparatus, and when problems arise they are apt to be construed as being due to 'operating difficulties' rather than to a need to rethink basic strategies. In the case of curriculum, the problem of the last hundred years has been one of access; the objects of policy have been the building of larger and more unified systems for delivering a curriculum to more and more students for a longer period of time. The very success of the vast mobilisation of resources that this has entailed has distracted attention from questions of the value of what the system is supposed to deliver. In terms of the data available for appraising the system, we have leaned heavily in the direction of information on inputs rather than outputs. We have even been distracted from studying what is happening within the system in our pursuit of a fixed goal relating to provision of places and equipment and to the encouragement of an ever-rising rate of enrolment. The virtual realisation of the goal, far from bringing us to a point of total problem solution, has left us facing crucial issues about what the curriculum should consist of, an almost total absence of means for resolving them, and a vast inertial educational system which would be desperately hard to reform, even if we knew how.

A particular factor in the decline of the ability to treat curriculum problems in the English school system has been the growth of what has been termed the 'educational sub-government'.[40] Educational problems have been regarded as issues which those professionally concerned should deal with. Teachers, local education authorities and the Department of Education and Science have joined together to form a closed context for defining the questions that should be asked and how they should be answered. Restriction on who should participate is inimical to good deliberation. The pool of ideas and perspectives is reduced, and the stimulus to search for comprehensive, relevant and accurate data is removed. It was not always so. Before the hundred-year expansion began, and during the early decades of its progress, deliberation about educational and curriculum decisions, as matters of public policy, were carried on with a higher regard for data, a greater sensitivity to the need for problem appreciation, and less restrictive attitude towards the range of views appropriate to adequate deliberation and judgment than we commonly find today. This is most obvious in the reports of the major nineteenth-century commissions. The Taunton Report of 1868 or the Bryce Report of 1895 are examples which illustrate the levels of practical reasoning that were achieved. In spite of the fact that they lacked the administrative and technical support that such bodies can call on today, the commissions nevertheless succeeded in gathering enormous quantities of information, in consulting the opinions of a wide range of people, and in profiting from studies of practice in other countries. Normally, the commissions met once or twice a week over a period of about two years. Much of this time was spent questioning and listening to witnesses from many walks of life who gave their opinions on what should be taught to whom, with what ends in view, and on what reforms and resources were needed to bring this about. But the commissions realised that one of their most major concerns should be with what already existed: with the present state of resources and with the existing outcomes of schooling. This they discovered by sending out assistant commissioners to visit schools and bring back detailed reports on their organisation and teaching. Information was also collected through questionnaires and sometimes the commissioners themselves visited schools. The Taunton Commission gathered evidence about the state of secondary education from hundreds of schools all over the country and published it in detail as part of the report. About six thick volumes are filled with the results of personal surveys and questionnaires. Day-by-day timetables are quoted, sometimes with notes of the texts studied in particular lessons. Examination papers are reproduced, with the marks gained on them by pupils. A similar number of volumes contain transcripts of interviews.

There are also accounts of studies of secondary education in Canada, the United States, France, Germany, Switzerland and Italy – the last four carried out for the Commission by Matthew Arnold. All these data are summed up in a single volume in which the main arguments as the commissioners saw them are deployed and recommendations made. Of course, their work displays some limitations inherent in the cultural context within which they were working. Students, for example, were not asked their opinion of what should be taught; the commissioners accepted without question that what should be taught was a function of the pupil's status in society; curriculum was thought of as a collection of basic skills and academic disciplines. But, though the prevailing culture of a society places limits on the possibilities that can be envisioned, this is only one determinant of the effectiveness of deliberation. It depends much more on how a task is conceptualized than on what resources of ideas and inventiveness exist for deliberation to uncover. In this respect the commissions showed a clear intuition of the nature of the practical reasoning that should be applied to curriculum problems. They saw that the problem was to envisage new states of the educational system that could be realised through adaptations to existing structures; they connected the question of what should be taught with the question of how it was to be achieved – what structures, what finance, what people would be needed; they distinguished and gave due importance to both the reality and the value judgment – 'The information we have collected ... falls naturally under two chief heads: first an account of what English secondary education now is; secondly, indications, more or less precise, of what it ought to be in order to meet the needs of the country and the wishes of parents.' The outcome of weighing this information was to be recommendations for adapting 'the schools to the work which is now required of them, by prescribing such a course of study as is needed by the country'. Above all, the publication of a full account of the evidence and the arguments provided a basis on which other people could form their own 'appreciations' of what exactly the problem about the secondary curriculum was.[41]

To contrast the report of the Taunton Commission with the recent Schools Council Working Party on *The Whole Curriculum 13–16*[42] may seem unfair to the latter: it was not set up by the Government with regal powers to command witnesses and resources, nor could it feel that it owed its existence to pressures of public demand and was working within a context of national political concern. Nevertheless, the title 'working party' should not obscure the fact that it had, for a full three years, the backing of a major public agency in the educational field, that it had sufficient standing to call on the services of leading experts and authorities, and that, compared to the nineteenth-century Commission, it could feel itself rich in the resources of research, theory and technical support to which it had access. But the real question is one of style and attitude: given that the Working Party had at least sufficient resources to construe its task in a variety of possible ways, how in fact did it construe it, and what attitude did it display towards the nature of curriculum problems and how they should be resolved? If this is taken to be the important question, then to use the report of the 13–16 Working Party is not an unfair index of the present state of curriculum deliberation in England.

The first point to note is the composition of the group. Of 35 members, 22 were head teachers, teachers or trainers of teachers. A further 8 were members of the Council staff whose experience lay largely in schools or in educational administration. The remaining 5 members were drawn from other parts of the educational service – the inspectorate, a university, further education, another administrator and the Director of the Council for Educational Technology. The membership was, then, wholly from the educational establishment, and, within that establishment, heavily weighted towards secondary heads and teachers (about 40 per cent, not including Council, college and university members whose main experience may have been in this field). Nor was the balance redressed by those listed as 'participants in special discussions'. Of these, 14 were members or ex-members of Schools Council subject committees, 4 from education departments, 2 from schools and 2 from the inspectorate. Only 3 were from other backgrounds. We would not be happy with having a committee to pronounce on the building of airports made up almost entirely of experts in aviation, or a committee to decide on where motorways should be constructed consisting mainly of highway engineers: why should we suppose that teachers are the only people who can tell us what kind of curriculum children should experience? But at least our experts in aviation, or our highway engineers, might have some special stock of knowledge that they could bring to bear on the problems at issue. The Working Party's report, on the other hand, explicitly states: 'Members ... were selected ... not because they would lay claim to any special expertise, but because of their long experience of secondary education.'[43] In other words, what was valued was not knowledge or study or research, but some lowest common denominator of conventional wisdom. At least the report writers show some consistency of ends and means in stating: 'This report is addressed mainly to teachers. ... [We] hope that many other people in the education service, *and indeed some outside it* will also find it of interest.'[44] Yet a 'paramount' aim of the Party's deliberation was, as expressed in the foreword to the Report, 'to ponder in depth the values on which the school curriculum rests'. How is this to be undertaken when those who are to ponder are those whose perceptions have been trained by active participation in the system?

Narrowness of view made problem appreciation a difficult task. There is no sense in this Report that deliberation can be a process of discovery – can take an existing situation and move it to a new plane of understanding and insight *before* an attempt is made to state what problems we ought to be trying to solve. They speak of 'trying to anticipate what readers would look for',[45] they subscribe to the kinds of orthodoxies that one would anticipate in a body of teachers ('We believe the improvement of the secondary-school curriculum must rest upon an acknowledgement of the central role of the teacher'[46]), and they assume the views already held in the group as fixed points and test how much consensus is possible: where it can be found, they make proposals, where it cannot they can only say that controversy exists. This made it very difficult for the group to decide exactly what problems it ought to try to solve: for the reader of the Report the object of deliberation begins to come into focus, fades, dissolves and then reappears in some different guise. Now we have solutions to things we did not know were problems, now problems with no sight of a solution. There is a general awareness that *something* is wrong with the 13–16 curriculum, but a distinct lack of ability to define what it is. But without a definition of this sort, of what use are solutions? To define problems we need data – opinions, but also facts. Here we have only opinions, and those drawn from a very restricted range of witnesses. Evidence of a harder kind is almost non-existent. In 116 pages of the Report, I can find only 4 references to factual data in quoted sources. The 1904 School Regulations are quoted on page 51; on page 25 a legal requirement of the 1944 Education Act is set out; on pages 29, 36 and 113 there are references to the Council's *Enquiry I*;[47] and on page 58 a book in the Council's Research Series is cited to point up sex differences in the curricula that students follow. Two of the *Enquiry I* references are to differences in teacher, pupil and parent perceptions of the aims of education, and the other is to pupils' reasons for staying in school after the statutory leaving age. A further 40 or so books, articles and pamphlets are referred to, but only to extract opinions or assertions. For example: 'The curriculum developers are the learners and the school is the teacher',[48] or, 'The examination and assessment system could provide an important tool for a more fully grounded evaluation of new curricula'.[49] About four of these other references could be taken as statements of theories, two make proposals for timetabling and one is to data that are available in a research study, but which are not specifically introduced into the argument of the Report. There is a handful of references to unpublished sources, including some to headmasters' accounts of how they plan their timetables.[50] There is nothing about what the present curriculum of 13–16-year-old pupils consists of, no evidence about how much commonality or variety exists, how many schools have undertaken innovatory courses or ways of structuring their curricula. Issues such as the introduction of integrated courses are discussed without any attempt to find out whether this is a serious problem in schools, how prevalent integration is or what forms it takes. The only hard statistic quoted on examinations is that 'The proportion of all school leavers who left in 1969–70 ... with one or more O-level or one or more CSE grade 5 or better was 54.9 per cent. ...' This figure was drawn from CBI evidence to the Working Party.[51] (Why does the Schools Council for the Curriculum *and Examinations* have to be told by the CBI how many children get examination qualifications?) I can find no mention at all of facts or experiences relating to foreign systems. The nearest approach to that is the listing on page 123 of I. J. Spitzburg Jnr of the Institute of Current World Affairs, New York, as a participant in a special discussion.

When we come to look at the Report in terms of the laying out of possibilities, the making of arguments for and against them and indications of what kinds of choice we should consider making, the quality of deliberation is equally poor. Argument and judgment yield place to assertion and the politics of consensus. The reader of the Report has no more knowledge, no more insight, no more sensitivity to the issues after sharing these deliberations than he had before; the problems are not defined, data are not provided and the grounds of argument not made clear. One can hardly, in this case, echo Vickers' summing up of the 1953 Report of the Royal Commission on Capital Punishment:

> The evidence on which the commissioners founded their reality judgment varies vastly in certainty and in character. Statistics and estimates; opinions, often discordant, on matters both of fact and value; the views of different authorities, past and present, on the legitimate purposes of punishment; the views of psychiatrists on human responsibility and its impairment by mental illness; all this and more goes into the mill and out comes the reality judgment, balanced, coherent, urbane, a mental artefact which only familiarity robs of the wonder which is its due.[52]

Here, as in the case of curriculum, there is conflict, uncertainty and problems of moral judgment. Their existence does not render problems intractable, though there is a dangerous doctrine, prevalent in education, that problems are intractable, and that one should subscribe to the positivist heresy that only that about which we have certain knowledge is debatable.

Uncertain practical problems are, by definition, hard to solve, but it is regrettable that such knowledge as we do have in the educational field about how to solve them is being allowed to wither away. For the decline in England in recent years, bodies such as the Schools Council and the DES must bear major responsibility. Both operate as part of the educational sub-government. The views of those outside the ranks of the providers of schools and curricula are seldom sought and even less frequently listened to. The possibility that anything can be learned by looking at foreign countries (even Scotland!) is almost totally ignored. A further downward twist has been given to the decline of the practical reasoning capacities of curriculum policy makers by the Council's ideological claim that only teachers can decide what should be taught – which is to say that problems of public interest which require for their statement and solution the participation of people and groups having a wide range of viewpoints and expertise should be settled by people having very particular opinions, attitudes and experience. Hence the Council's inability to engage in discussion of what is desirable, and its eagerness to reduce questions of what is desirable to questions of what is possible. From this propensity stems the so-called 'feasibility study', now elevated to a new height of incredibility in the 'theoretical feasibility studies' carried out on the new proposals for sixth form syllabuses. In this exercise groups were convened to write courses to answer curriculum problems which have never been adequately defined and say how 'feasibly' they could be implemented in schools, without actually trying to implement them. The underlying assumptions are that the context of the school must be accepted as a 'given' in any proposal for change, and that nothing must actually change, even experimentally, unless teachers want it to. It is against this background that statements about conflicting aims and the difficulty of securing consensus must be viewed. Bodies responsible for advising governments on curriculum should engage in serious efforts to raise the level of problem appreciation, not leave it bogged down in questions of 'feasibility' and in discussion papers that are founded on a thin and narrow data base, as the Council does, nor shuffle it to one side as the DES has recently shown itself inclined to do by weighing in with its own predetermined solutions, in advance of any problem identification, and promulgating them in papers equally devoid of the substance of reality judgment, but, in this instance, not even open to public view.[53]

The problem is not just that curriculum questions are being badly handled, but that the means of handling them well is being steadily eroded, for the exercise of practical reasoning depends on the existence of a living tradition. Once we have found ways of treating procedural questions, they will continue to be available to us; formulae and techniques, once discovered, stay discovered, short of natural catastrophe. But the methods of practical reasoning have to be learned through experience and involvement, and live and die with the individuals who exercise them. Vickers puts it as follows:

> Those who are engaged in a course of decision-making soon become aware that each decision is conditioned not only by the concrete situation in which it is taken but also by the sequence of past decisions; and that their new decisions in their turn will influence future decisions not only by their effect on the history of events but also by the precedents which they set.[54]

Thus the context within which initiatives can be exercised is constantly changing and 'scope for initiative is created and preserved largely by the way in which it is exercised. It follows that good judgment can be recognised only over a span of years. Tomorrow is already committed; but how varied, today, are the possibilities for ten, twenty, thirty years hence!'[55]

Seeing curriculum problems as uncertain practical problems that have to be treated by the exercise of practical reasoning has a number of healthy results for curriculum theory and practice. From the point of view of theory, it saves curriculum thinking from the blind alleys of unwarranted seeking after science on the one hand, and denial that it can be anything more than common sense on the other. It allows curriculum theory to cohere round a special set of problems that demand a knowledge of specific kinds of contexts, data and understandings, but which, at the same time, can be seen as part of a wider group of uncertain practical problems with social and moral significance. The curriculum thinker and the curriculum maker are not cut off from others who should contribute to the solution of curriculum problems as they are when curriculum theory is construed as a special kind of applied technology available only to initiates.[56] From the point of view of practice, we benefit from the acknowledgment that curriculum problems do not admit of ideal solutions, from the return to a central place in decision-making of commitment and responsibility, and from the realisation that the exercise of practical reason is only to be justified in *action*. Too often curriculum decision-making has suffered from the illusion that there must be a uniquely 'right' answer to a problem. The search is conceptualised as an attempt to discover what already exists. If it cannot be found, the problem is: (1) left unsolved, or (2) it is 'solved' by setting up a treatment with the same name as the problem, or (3) it is handed over to the 'technical experts'. An example of the first type of outcome is the treatment of the problem of the sixth form curriculum by the Schools Council. A ten-year search for a non-existent 'uniquely right' formula has stifled the possibility of progress and students are therefore condemned to a set of outdated learning experiences, even though a great deal might have been done to improve the curriculum within its present framework.[57] An example of the second outcome is the attempt by the Council to treat the problem of the relation of the curriculum to industry by having an 'Industry' project, on the supposition that giving the right name to the remedy is equivalent to solving the problem.[58] The third type of outcome is illustrated by the initiative of the DES in 'solving' the problem of the adequacy of basic skills learning by setting up an 'Assessment of Performance Unit' to produce basic skills tests.[59] A further weakness in decision-making has been the flight from values and commitments. Partly this has resulted from a praiseworthy desire to save education from becoming indoctrination, but greater significance is to be attached to two further factors: first, the decline in the wish and the ability to engage in debates on values that results from a narrow definition of the range of those deemed competent to take part (since it is an invitation to 'outsiders' to join in) and second, a belief that the need to take up and defend value positions has somehow been reduced by the development of technical and procedural expertise. But technique and procedure are not, in their application, value-free and to believe that they are is to abandon the exercise of responsible choice that is inseparable from the justification of curriculum decisions. When expertise in solving curriculum problems is seen as part of a wider range of expertise in which all are to some degree competent, then the way becomes clearer to making curricula responsive to varied and changing social needs. If curriculum problems are seen as technical problems that can only be solved by those with inside knowledge of schools or of curriculum design, then it is hardly surprising that outsiders are found to have little to contribute. But if the scope of appreciative and judgmental processes is widened, and if the activities of appreciation and judgment are set up to be intrinsically educative, then the problem of breadth of participation seems not so daunting. Finally, the realisation that practical problems are solved only in action puts into a new light questions of why decisions are not effectively implemented, or why curriculum materials fail to get adopted. The technical model of treating curriculum problems suggests that failure must lie in the schools – 'Let's go and see why these people are not doing what they should be, or what we hoped they would.' The practical reasoning model suggests that if the problem is not being solved in action, then the process through which the action was decided on was perhaps at fault. Why should we suppose that setting up a curriculum project will solve a curriculum problem? Perhaps a more adequate problem appreciation would have indicated other possible courses of action. And whatever action we choose should be chosen through a deliberate process that takes account of data and judgments on the likely *effects* of the various courses we might pursue, not just through looking at their procedural feasibility.[60]

Apart from these directly instrumental advantages, the practical reasoning approach can offer a wider range of benefits than the approach through technique and procedure. The latter offers advantages only in terms of its products, and if these are unsuccessful the gains of using it are confined to the experts who were hired to carry out the work. The former offers advantages that accrue from the process as well as the product. The process educates the participants and improves the general level of problem appreciation, even when solutions are elusive or ineffective. It develops skills of general, not merely specific use, and thereby increases the ability of the educational system and the wider community to be sensitive to and to treat curriculum problems. By stressing key words like 'action', 'judgment', 'deliberation', 'appreciation', 'criticism', 'responsibility', 'argument' and 'justification' it introduces a fresh and more appropriate climate of metaphor into curriculum theory and practice which may help us to avoid the kinds of errors into which we are led by thinking in the imagery of engineering and design. We may draw a parallel with Kaplan's observation that 'Aesthetics does not produce art, but it may free both artist and audience from constraints that stand in the way of its creation and appreciation.'[61] In this way too, practical reasoning may justify itself through the process of its application and not merely through its immediate and visible products.

5 The problem of curriculum change

Advocacy of practical reasoning as a means of solving curriculum problems implies acceptance of the proposition that changes in what is taught and how it is taught can be brought about in planned ways, or at least that this is to an important degree possible. It also implies that the nature of curriculum change is such that, of a variety of approaches to planned change which might be supported, this one is most likely to be effective in defining and realising curricular purposes. Arguments of this type touch on an area of deep controversy with far-reaching implications for the theory and practice of curriculum. The two basic points at issue are: can change be in any fundamental sense planned, or is the evolution of the curriculum determined by social forces that tend in a particular and irreversible direction? And must proposals for curriculum change be based on some set of values, or some ideological[1] position, or can they be, in some sense, 'value free'? The approach through practical reasoning accepts that planning is possible and that it must reflect ideological commitments. Two other, importantly different, views of curriculum change are to be found in the literature of curriculum theory. For convenience of exposition, they are presented here in their extreme forms. The first claims that intentionality is indeed (or can be) the dominant factor in curriculum change, but assumes that a theory of practice can be non-ideological. This is the position of writers of the school of Bobbitt and Tyler[2] who deploy a 'managerial' perspective on curriculum theory. Management is, by definition, capable of being effective, but what management achieves is thought of as politically and ideologically neutral. The second view claims that any attempt to intervene in curriculum matters must be politically and ideologically motivated, but that the changes that actually take place are attributable more to socio-cultural necessity than to the realisation of freely chosen goals through managerial intervention. This view is implied in the statements of writers such as Young and Kallós.[3] When the argument is joined from the extreme positions, both sides are fairly invulnerable to the thrusts of the other, and the possibilities for achieving a synthesis are limited. The 'intentionalists' cannot attack the 'inevitablists' for being just as ideologically motivated as everyone else without admitting that they themselves are ideologically motivated, while the latter cannot mount substantial arguments against interventionism without admitting that it may be effective – which they deny.[4] Of course, many theorists, while tending towards one view or the other, avoid the extreme and put forward views which are not obviously incompatible with either position. Sometimes, even, extremists of both types will find themselves on the same side, as, for example, in denunciations of the arguments of the proponents of 'de-schooling', which suggests that their views are not diametrically opposed. Both positions contain worthwhile insights, but they also contain some serious theoretical and practical flaws.

Some theoretical deficiencies of the 'managerial' approach have been succinctly documented by Kliebard[5] who points to its inability to give anything like an adequate account of where the objectives of the curriculum are derived from.

> The crucial first step in the Tyler rationale on which all else hinges is the statement of objectives. The objectives are to be drawn from three sources: studies of the learner, studies of society, and suggestions from subject matter specialists. Data drawn from these sources are to be filtered through philosophical and psychological screens. Upon examination, the last of the three sources turns out to be no source at all but a means of achieving objectives drawn from the other two. Studies of the learner and of society depend so heavily for their standing as sources on the philosophical screen that it is actually the philosophical screen that determines the nature and scope of the objectives. To say that educational objectives are drawn from one's philosophy, in turn, is only to say that one must make choices about educational objectives in some way related to one's value structure. This is to say so little about the process of selecting objectives as to be virtually meaningless.[6]

But these are not deficiencies to be repaired by some reformulation of the theory that leaves its basic assumptions intact. Writers such as Inglis and Booth[7] have argued persuasively that the whole notion that policies with social consequences can be set up in some apolitical way is a dangerous nonsense. In the case of curriculum, we are talking about the distribution of advantage and disadvantage in society through the differential provision of opportunities to acquire knowledge or to acquire the status that goes with having been exposed to certain kinds of knowledge. There is no question of simply doing it more or less 'effectively'. 'Effectiveness' in such a situation only has a meaning when it relates to some set of recognised ideals or values.

On a practical level, the weaknesses of the traditional managerial approach are that the process it proposes is not one that curriculum designers find natural,[8] and that it has little to say about how a curriculum design should be implemented, so that innovations which rely on this model may be ineffective in practice.[9] Nevertheless, the shortcomings of this branch of curriculum theory should not disguise the fact that its progenitors were inspired by an idea that was fundamentally right – that it is the business of curriculum theory to try to say something about how, practically, curriculum tasks such as design, implementation and evaluation can and should be carried out.

Writers of the opposite persuasion tend to avoid the discussion of effective practices, and may go so far as to claim that nothing much can be said about curriculum change either.

> Academic theorists, often in search of a spurious scientism, can be far more naive than teachers. They present curriculum as a reality to which the language of cause and effect, resistance and change, is appropriate, and we discover articles with absurd titles like 'How does the curriculum change?'[10]

Those who like to make such statements can always know that they are logically unassailable. Hume showed conclusively that, if we wish to push logic to its limits, the language of cause and effect cannot be applied to anything, whether it be the curriculum, the physical universe or the writing of articles on the evils of using cause-effect language. Obstinately, however, academics, planners and ordinary citizens have carried on using such language, first, because most do not have access to any other language that could replace it, and second, because the asking of how and why questions, and the attempts to answer them, are useful ways of increasing our stock of perceptions, capabilities and understandings. This is not to advocate simplistic analyses of curriculum change of the 'causes of the French Revolution' type, but to accept a commitment to a view of human affairs which allows a place for choice and responsibility, and to a view of intellectual enquiry that, instead of placing of limits on the permitted means for producing ideas and theories, stresses the critical evaluation of those ideas and theories once they have been formulated. The fact that no conclusive arguments can be put forward for the operation of cause and effect does not logically entail the acceptance of determinism, neither is there any proven argument against determinism: whichever side of the controversy is espoused, it is on the basis of the acceptance of some world view. What would be logically unacceptable would be to argue that the curriculum is capable of responding to the intentional interventions of planners of various kinds, whether classroom teachers or central administrators, and at the same time to deny that such interventions reflected any kind of ideological or political stance. This is where the 'inevitablists' are right: all attempted intervention is on the basis of value commitments, explicit or implicit. Their mistake is to suppose that a deterministic view of curriculum change can be presented as ideologically neutral. The starting point for the present enquiry is the belief that there are certain kinds of activity that one studies because of a commitment to the proposition that they are capable of producing worthwhile effects, and that planning curriculum change is an activity of this type. The practical, and undesirable, result of a determinist view of change is that decision-makers must regard themselves as ineffectual or, alternatively, as effective only in acting as agents for power groups. Either way, they are denied any sense that they might be able to act constructively or responsibly.

Functional and conflict theories

To pursue an enquiry into curriculum change we do not need to debate lengthily about whether curriculum is or is not a 'reality' (any more than the exponents of determinism need, for their purposes, to consider whether 'capitalism' or 'socialism' are 'realities'). The focus of interest is on what is learned; the factors which promote the type of learning that takes place, or which lead to changes in types or patterns of learning are allowed, initially, to be problematic. They may take the form of things which can be objectively studied and described – the architecture of the school or the textbooks and teachers' guides that form the physical manifestation of a curriculum design – or they may be less tangible elements, such as the social relationships that exist between teachers and taught, or the implicit or explicit theories about the nature of children and learning that guide the activities of educators. The looseness of definition is deliberate. Several decades of experience of the managerial model should have resulted in at least one useful outcome: an appreciation of the danger of working with a tight definition of curriculum when our interest is not in making a theoretical point, but in providing grounds for the development of theories of effective practice to guide the conduct of curriculum tasks.

Most learning which can be associated with the notion of curriculum takes place in 'open' systems. That is, parameters cannot be set and controlled so that learning outcomes are associated with selected stimuli. How the stimulus is applied is a matter of the beliefs and skills of the teacher, how children respond is a matter of the background and interests of the student. But, beyond this, the learning takes place in a situation that is not adapted to one way stimulus-response processes: as well as being a place for learning, the classroom is a place where long-term interactive relationships have to be managed, and a place where the needs of individuals intersect with the organisational imperatives of institutions. Schools are not efficient delivery systems for a particular kind of goods, they are cultures promoted as an act of public policy in the belief that their existence will increase and enrich the stock of such goods in the community. Curriculum change is, therefore, a species of socio-cultural change.[11] Adoption of this view leads us away from those types of enquiry (psychology, some types of history) that place the individual in the centre of the stage, and towards those that stress the group, the culture or the organisation (anthropology, social psychology, organisational analysis, political theory). Theories of socio-cultural change stemming from these traditions of thought can be divided into two broad categories: functional theories and conflict theories.

The basic position of the functionalist is well stated by Silverman:

> Functionalism begins with Hobbes' problem of order and proceeds to ask some important and interesting questions. 'How is it' functionalists would ask, 'that society manages to work and to survive continual changes of personnel? How do people with different genetic make-ups and personality types learn to co-exist with one another and even enter into more or less stable and predictable forms of relationship?' In answering these questions, functionalists take as their concern the relationship of the parts to the whole in order to show how what appear to be isolated, if not inexplicable, social phenomena may fulfil some wider purpose related to the stability of society. Thus, their perspective ... generates a concern with the causes and consequences of social equilibrium; problems of change and conflict, while they are considered, are treated as subsidiary phenomena.[12]

Supporters of conflict theory would criticise this approach as allowing too little place for concepts such as power, and as preempting the question of what makes for change by seeing everything in terms of stability: 'since this situation exists, it exists necessarily and the task is to show why'. Such a position, they would maintain, naturally reinforces dominant ideologies and particularly those that delay the realisation of goals such as the reduction or removal of social class differences. Conflict theorists would prefer to regard what exists as the result of the exercise of power, and to see change as resulting from the shifting balances between groups in society which compete for the opportunity to exercise power. Since the examples to be given later in this essay take a broadly functionalist view of what a theory of curriculum change might look like, it may be useful at this point to provide an instance of the kind of argument that a conflict perspective might produce, and to draw from it some conclusions about the relative advantages of the two kinds of approach and about the extent to which they may be complementary or compatible.

If we accept that socio-cultural change results from the shifting distribution of power between competing groups in society, then the evolution of the curriculum of the English public school[13] can be seen as a series of responses to the influence exerted over it by social classes which used their political power to attempt to change the way in which the benefits of public school education were made available. First, in the early nineteenth century, the commercial upper middle classes laid claim to the services of the public school which, until then, had been the preserve of the landed aristocracy. But, in gaining acceptance, they imported into the schools a more utilitarian approach to the curriculum, backed up by an ethos that stressed protestant, capitalist values. The response of the school was to offer, not a completely new curriculum, but an alternative curriculum, and the system grew up of choice between classical, 'modern' or scientific studies which has moulded the whole of the secondary curriculum to the present day. Later, towards the end of the century, the public schools were conscious of the growing power of the lower classes whose ideologies could not be accommodated to theirs. By the time of the 1902 Education Act there was real anxiety among public school headmasters that such schools would shortly disappear. The conflict was not now about access to the schools, but about their right to exist at all, since they served to reinforce the dominance of the classes which already controlled the major power centres of society. The response of the schools this time was to play down their distinctiveness, to match their curricula more closely to those of the new secondary schools that were being set up under state control after the passing of the 1902 Education Act. At the same time, supporters of the public schools infiltrated the state system both as heads and as high-level administrators to make sure that the matching problem would not be made too great through the adoption of radical curriculum proposals for the new maintained schools. In more recent times, the public schools have gone further, and taken the lead in curriculum development projects aimed at state schools. They were pioneers in Nuffield Science schemes and new approaches to language learning, and were prime movers in the 'General Studies' movement.

The general drift of this kind of analysis shows up one important difference between it and functional theory as a means of understanding curriculum change. Several different interpretations of the nature of curriculum knowledge can be fitted to a functional theory, including one which would regard it as in some way 'objective',[14] but conflict theory seems to involve, necessarily, a relativist view of curriculum knowledge. Since the control of the curriculum is a political objective to be won, the knowledge which it represents is a good to be contested. The classroom is a battleground in which conflicting stocks of knowledge confront one another. What the knowledge consists of is almost irrelevant. The point is that it should be valued by some and coveted or despised by others. It is an instrument of political domination, or revolutionary guerrilla warfare. If we think that knowledge can never under any circumstances be free from political implications, then the question of what should be taught becomes a matter of whose version of 'truth' is politically dominant; since knowledge is a symbol or instrument of political supremacy, what we teach is a matter of fashion. To take the contrary view and assert that there *is* such a thing as objective knowledge is not to say that *all* knowledge, and especially curriculum knowledge, is objectively true or intrinsically worthwhile. We can still admit that some knowledge enters into the curriculum for political reasons, or that the choice of methods or materials can have political bias, such as the use of 'middle-class' story books in the teaching of reading to 'disadvantaged' children. But acceptance of the possibility of objective knowledge provides a ground for building a tradition of critical argument about what should be in a curriculum which represents something more than just the manoeuvrings of power groups.

A second feature of conflict theory in its more extreme forms is that it allows little or no room for the exercise of judgment and responsibility in planning or policy making. Social change, and therefore curriculum change, is depicted as something hinging on fundamental social conflicts over which we have only very marginal control, though we might be able to slow the process down or speed it up. This might be said to be true also of the extreme functionalist view: to account for a state of affairs in terms of massively interlocking component features of a society is to suggest that such systems are self-regulating and totally resistant to purposeful intervention. The difference is that functional theory does not claim that the equilibrium it describes is the only one that could exist, or that any given state of the system has a necessarily antecedent or successor. If more than one state of a system is possible, it is equally possible that we could manage a transition from one to another and choose this other from a range of feasible states. In suggesting that this may be a difficult process, the functional theorist is reflecting the reality of actual experience of curriculum design. (One does not find writers complaining that curricula are difficult to plan and manage because they are so volatile: on the contrary, many books are written to show that curricula have a great tendency to move inexorably along established paths in spite of all the efforts of planners to deflect them.[15]) But this is not the same thing as saying that they never could be changed in consciously and rationally chosen ways,[16] and functionalist accounts can suggest methods by which change can be secured. Conflict theories, on the other hand, while they are concerned to highlight questions of change, rather than documenting grounds for stability, tend not to point to ways in which responsible intervention can take place, because it is a basic premise of such theories either that this kind of intervention is not possible or that it has to be directed towards the achievement of goals that are known in advance of discussion or action. A conflict-centred account of curriculum change in the English public school does not suggest that options existed, or that at certain points a rational choice between options could have been exercised. In what ways is such an analysis helpful to anyone wanting to make and implement such choices? It documents a change process in such a way that a dramatic meaning is given to events in the schools, and relationships between these and forces outside the school are suggested (a valuable and necessary exercise); but the documentation is of a process that is accepted as basically inevitable and the meanings arise from a presumed knowledge of future states of the school and the surrounding society.

The kinds of problems raised here about the practical utility and the explanatory power of functional and conflict theories arise only if these are presented as mutually exclusive and incompatible sources of knowledge. This is how they have, in fact, been put forward by some writers, but others have provided arguments for supposing that this need not and should not be the case.[17] Fallding expresses the point very strongly: 'It has been very common ... to oppose a Marxian-type "conflict" sociology to a "functionalist" sociology. But that is dealing in stereotypes in the most puerile way.'[18] We need to see the two types of approach either as equally capable of providing useful insights or as capable of integration: though they may seem incompatible, this need not be a reason for choosing one against the other: 'we need for the explanation of sociological problems, both the equilibrium and the conflict models of society ... there is no intrinsic criterion for preferring the one to the other.'[19] And, as Gouldner points out: 'A way of seeing is also a way of not seeing.' Those who are interested primarily in the practical consequences of understanding change processes will subscribe to whatever ways of seeing are open to them. But such a pragmatic approach may not be necessary. Fallding suggests that a broadly defined functionalism can accommodate change mechanisms which are conflict related. A functionalist theory has somehow to account for the fact that what was stable at some time in the past has been replaced by an apparent present stability of a different nature. This it does by recognising that if function is a viable concept, then the concept of dysfunction must also be accepted. Dysfunction will cause stress and pressure for change to establish a new functional equilibrium. There is no reason to suppose that conflict between social groups will not be an important factor in the creation and the resolution of dysfunction.[20] In this way, discussion of aims and purposes can be imported into functionalist paradigms. Deliberation will be the means by which tensions are resolved through a choice of a future system state which is attainable and which respects the aims and purposes of the participants. Functionalism can be seen as a 'capacious position', or a 'program of inquiry' rather than a strictly delineated conceptual position.[21]

The major charge that can be laid against functionalism is that it is too loosely formulated and therefore open to a wide variety of interpretations and to misuse in support of a range of *a priori* positions.

There is some justice in this criticism, but, as has been suggested earlier, the validity of enquiry is assured not by the refinement of conceptual tools, but the rigorous scrutiny of the ideas that these tools produce. And this will be a particularly telling point for those whose main concern is with gaining understandings of social change that could have some practical usefulness. For whatever theory of change we put forward, and however broadly the definition of function is drawn, the account given will be partial and incomplete. Criteria have to be found for evaluating such theories. Among these might be questions such as: are the elements chosen in such a way that they reflect the results of empirical study? Do they have common sense as well as theoretical significance? Does the theory show schools in terms of similarities with other organisations as well as in terms of uniqueness? Does the theory indicate how those interested in planned change could better understand their failures and their successes?

To ask that empirical study should be reflected in theory is not to ask that it should be empirically validated. It is impossible to 'prove' or 'disprove' social theory by the amassing of facts. Such theories remain, essentially, 'ways of seeing'. But the scope for producing theoretical formulations is endless unless some empirical base is respected, and the multiplication of analytical proposals does not make for a coherent tradition of thought in a practical field. Practical concerns are also the reason for wanting theoretical elements to have commonsense significance. If they cannot be described in such a way that they can be recognised by teachers and administrators, then it is unlikely that they adequately reflect those aspects of schools and curricula that could be of use in planning change. But, at the same time, we should be suspicious of theories of the school and the curriculum that seem to bear no relation to theoretical formulations about other kinds of social institutions. A curriculum must in some ways be a unique phenomenon, but in others it must participate in the features of other comparable phenomena. A theory of curriculum change should be one of a family of change theories. Finally, it is a consequence of the interpretation of curriculum theory that is being adopted here that a theory of change should have implications for theories of effective practice.

A theory of curriculum change

The following discussion is intended not to present a final and conclusive theoretical account oı curriculum change, but to put forward an example of functional analysis that tries to meet the criteria stated above. The starting point is evidence collected in primary and secondary schools about how teachers see the forces that determine what is taught and how it is taught. This evidence is limited, in that it represents only one point of view and also in that it is based on questionnaire surveys involving short response scales or 'yes-no' answers. The data on the primary curriculum were provided by 120 teachers in 12 West Midland schools.[22] Their answers to a set of questions about constraints on the achievement of curricular aims were factored and three main dimensions identified relating to: (i) resources and facilities in the school; (ii) children's attitudes, backgrounds and experience; (iii) aspects of relationships among staff. Consideration of the defining variables of these factors suggested that they might represent some of the features of functional models of organisations that recognise three main internal elements, usually described as 'technology', 'social systems' and 'theory' (or aims) (see Table 1). Factor (i) could be seen as reflecting 'technology' and factor (iii) the 'social system'. Factor (ii) might relate to inputs to the organisation. No such theory had been considered in devising questions, which had been suggested by teachers, but some confirmation of its appropriateness was to be found in responses to other item sets on aims and influences. What was missing was any indication of an 'output' factor to balance the 'input' one, and any factor relating to 'theory' – that is to how the task of the school was conceptualised by the teachers. These were not found because none of the questions related to them. The omissions were repaired in a later survey of sixth form teachers.[23] Replies from 194 individuals in 31 schools yielded factors which confirmed the tentative model derived from the primary school data, and enabled it to be elaborated and extended. This time factors obtained from replies on both constraints and influences could be combined into a single theoretical formulation which is shown in Figure 2. The teacher advisory groups which had helped to plan the research recognised in the factors a reflection of their own perceptions of the ways in which the curriculum was determined. The model did not enforce a conceptualisation of questions about schools and curricula identical to that which might have been employed for other types of institution, but it did employ elements which had been found appropriate in other contexts.

Simply stated, the model represents the curriculum as, in some of its major aspects, the resultant of a balance that exists between three salient features of the school as an organisation – technology, social system and theory. This balance is affected by inputs to and outputs from the school, in the form of entering and leaving students, and by social forces operating outside the school, either in the form of specific institutions, or the generally available stock of ideas, attitudes and values. Whatever is outside the school is marked off from it by a boundary which in specific instances may be of greater or lesser strength. Technology here does not refer simply to actual equipment that may be used in teaching. It follows rather Perrow's definition of 'a technique or complex of techniques employed to alter "materials" (human or non-human, mental or physical) in an anticipated manner'.[24] It is the means that an organisation

Table 1 *Factor analyses of constraints on teaching**

1 Technology		*2 Social System*	
(Primary teachers)		(Primary)	
Provision of ancillary help	0.83†	Co-operation between staff	0.77
Provision of specialist facilities	0.70	Style of discipline	0.76
Provision of teaching materials	0.51	Readiness of staff to give time to preparing work	0.68
Provision of storage space	0.45	Quality of communication	0.32
(Sixth form teachers)		(Sixth form)	
Layout and equipment of class rooms	0.78	Level of assistance in planning syllabuses	0.70
Level of knowledge of pupils	0.60	Degree of communication and co-operation between teachers	0.61
Time available for finding out about teaching methods	0.53	Agreement within school about aims	0.59
Level of provision – library, private study facilities	0.51	Expectation of other members of staff about subject	0.55

3 Input		*4 Output*	
(Primary)		(Sixth form)	
Attitudes of children	0.77	Requirements of employers	0.66
Children's home environment	0.74	Local education committee policies	0.65
Abilities of children	0.69	Attitudes of parents to sixth form education	0.65
Children's previous experience	0.50	Content of university courses	0.64
(Sixth form)			
Range of abilities among pupils	0.83		
Home background of sixth formers	0.70		
Content of course followed by pupils to O-level	0.62		

5 Theory	
(Sixth form)	
Content of A-level syllabuses	0.79
Problems of evaluating the effectiveness of teaching	0.77
Your own qualifications	0.72
University admissions policies	0.53

* Sources: P. H. Taylor *et al.*, *Purpose, Power and Constraint in the Primary School Curriculum*, London, Macmillan, 1974, pp. 31–37 and P. H. Taylor *et al.*, *The English Sixth Form: A Case Study in Curriculum Research*, London, Routledge & Kegan Paul, 1974, pp. 99–101. † Loadings of variables on varimax factors.

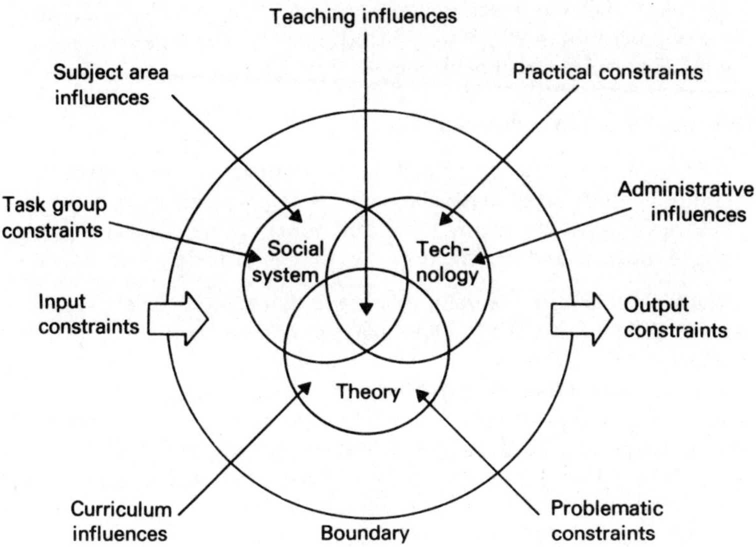

Figure 2 A functional model of the school (after P. H. Taylor *et al.*, *The English Sixth Form: A Case Study in Curriculum Research*, London, Routledge & Kegan Paul, 1974, Figure 1, p. 102)

employs to get its work done. To an extent, the curriculum *is* the technology of the school – the means of achieving the task it sets out to do. But it is not only that. What is learned in school is also a resultant of the set of relationships that holds between teachers and teachers, students and students and teachers and students, and of notions of the task of the school that may be only implicitly held and not deliberately expressed through the curriculum. It is through the social system that the technology of the organisation is implemented; in the case of schools, principally by the teachers, administrators and ancillary helpers. But sometimes students are held responsible for their own learning, or work collaboratively with teachers. They themselves then belong to that part of the social system that operates as a task group. Theory, like technology, is used in a somewhat technical sense to mean how the nature of the task is defined. In the case of schools, what do they exist for? What kinds of learning should they promote? How do children learn? What constitutes appropriate behaviour on the part of teachers and children? Sometimes, these questions may be formally posed and considered. But they do not have to be verbalised in order that a 'theory' of the institution can exist. Whatever activities it engages in, these will betray the existence of implicitly held beliefs about teaching, learning and task of the school. Using a slightly different terminology, Perrow sums up these propositions as follows:

> Organisations are influenced by three factors: the cultural system which sets legitimate goals, the technology which determines the

> means available for reaching these goals, and the social structure of the organisation in which specific techniques are embedded in such a way as to permit goal achievement.[25]

This may be compared to Sorokin's:

> All empirically rooted socio-cultural phenomena are made up of three components: 1. meanings-values-norms; 2. physical and biological vehicles objectifying them; 3. mindful human beings (and groups) that create, operate and use them in the process of their interaction.[26]

Many writers at the present time argue that schools reflect society at large.[27] Broadly speaking, the analysis offered here supports this conclusion. Whatever technologies, relationships or theories exist in schools are found there because they are drawn from a stock of models available in society. It does not follow, however, that in what the school does it must necessarily adopt whatever is currently the dominant model. It may use models which elsewhere are falling from favour, or it may incorporate ideas and behaviours which are characteristic of minority groups. The theoretical approach proposed here can help understanding of the circumstances under which one situation or the other tendency will occur or can be encouraged to occur.

The choices open to the school are practically limited by the propensity towards the establishment of equilibria between technology, task group and theory, and between the school and the surrounding environment. Change comes about mainly through the operation of external forces which tend to act differentially on the three elements of the organisation. Equilibrium may be restored through a return of that element to its former state. In that case, the change is only temporary. An example would be where an 'integrated' curriculum is introduced but purely in terms of technology without compensating movement in theory or social system. For a while the curriculum is implemented, but only because teachers are prepared to expend extra energy in overcoming the inertial effects of a theory and social system that are incompatible with integration. Eventually, the inertial forces gain the upper hand and, though the semblance of the innovation may be preserved, there is a reversion to the roles of subject specialists teaching self-contained courses.[28] Very often the return to the previous equilibrium follows on an attempt to change some part of the technology of the school,[29] for this is the most likely element to be open to immediate influence from external commercial and political pressures. Disused language laboratories, didactically taught discussion and discovery materials, unstreaming accompanied by rapid growth in 'remedial' classes are all results of initiatives that brought new technology to schools without effecting fundamental and lasting change in the curriculum.[30]

Sometimes, however, the forces of change act on all three elements, or the other elements move to adjust themselves to the one affected by an innovation. A new form of curriculum is then institutionalised. This is most likely to happen when a change takes place in the theory of the school. There is then a commitment on the part of the task group to new goals and a willingness to explore and experiment in order to find ways of achieving them. Changing beliefs about the nature of young children and the nature of the learning process have been accompanied by the development in many first schools of methods of team teaching and discovery learning that have enabled these beliefs to be lastingly reflected in the curriculum.[31]

We can now postulate that the curriculum offered by the school will be to a great extent dependent on:

(i) the stocks of knowledge, ideas, images, styles and models available in its environment (for most schools, in society at large);
(ii) the nature of the input of students it receives;
(iii) the nature of the output of students (their destinations);
(iv) the influence channelled towards the school by other institutions;
(v) the strength of the boundary around the school;
(vi) the need for congruence between theory, social system and technology within the school;
(vii) the need for congruence between the activities of the school and the demands of outside forces.

Each of these factors will be briefly considered, and indications given of how they act to influence the kinds of curricula which schools offer.

Factors influencing the form of the curriculum

A major limiting factor on the form of any particular curriculum is the variety of models available to influence it. Models relevant to the shaping of curricula are:

(i) models of the nature of knowledge and knowing;
(ii) models of truth-seeking strategies within the subjects to be taught;
(iii) models of the nature of children;
(iv) models of desirable adult characteristics;
(v) models of relationships between people and particularly between adults and children;
(vi) models of the role of the teacher and of effective teaching;
(vii) models of the curriculum itself.

Fundamental to any consideration of why curricula take the forms they do is the question, what ways of conceptualising the nature of knowledge and the process of acquiring it exist in the surrounding society? And to what extent are these available for inclusion in the theory of the school? Schools do not necessarily have to wait until ideas about learning are generally accepted before adopting them, but there has to be some degree of acceptance of them before they can be successfully incorporated. Exactly how far they have to spread before they become influential on schools will depend on the strength of the boundary between the school and the outside world and on the school's relationship to institutions that generate and diffuse ideas on knowledge and learning. If a stage has not yet been reached when there are generally available technologies and social systems to support the theory, then disequilibrium and rejection may result. It is often the case that the school is operating on a theory of knowledge which, though popularly held, is rejected by philosophers and psychologists. Teaching continues to be dominated in most schools by passive models of knowledge acquisition based on a 'naive theory of vision'. According to this,

> the eye does not contribute anything to the object seen; it simply registers the object. Similarly, when understanding is treated as a kind of seeing, the mind simply registers the idea. ... It follows from the supposed passivity of the eye that the object seen is wholly there, with all its *visual* properties, colour, shape, size. It exists prior to the act of seeing, and is unaffected by the act of seeing. ... The vision-based theory of understanding states that direct inspection, or intuition, results in clear ideas. ... Common-sense theories of understanding are still based on common-sense theories of seeing.[32]

The content of the curriculum will reflect the range of knowledge thought to be important and, in the case of academic 'subjects', the way they are conceived and practised in industry, higher education or learned societies. The biology curriculum in the nineteenth century had to be 'taxonomic' in character because that was the state of the research paradigm on which it was modelled.[33] Chemistry, on the other hand, presented several different possibilities, but it was the one subscribed to by those high in the social structure of the discipline that became almost universally adopted.[34] Recent curriculum reform movements have been concerned to persuade schools to respond to alternative models, either because they are clinging to an outdated conception of the 'approved' model, or in order to promote the acceptance of a variety of models capable of serving a wider range of purposes. Examples would be the introduction of new science curricula. The early Nuffield schemes in England were indicators to the schools that science's image of itself was changing and that more emphasis should be placed on the innovative rather than the normative aspects of scientific activity. Later projects were more concerned with suggesting roles for school science other than that of inducting students into science as a professional activity.[35]

Though the nineteenth century generally saw children as subordinate creatures, in need of moral correction and inspiration, and having to be disciplined in order to be taught, notions of the child as autonomous learner were not lacking. However, their entry into the language of educators and teachers was a very gradual process which can be charted through analysis of the language of official reports.[36] Similarly, there are, at any time, a variety of images of the desirable adults that children, as a result of education, should grow into, and of the relations that should exist between children and adults. The view that is projected in the school may be one that relates to a particular section of society, if that is what the school serves, or it may be one that is widely accepted. A few schools deliberately set out to promote models which are not generally admired.[37] An example of shifts in the accepted models of behaviour on the part of children and adults, and of relations between them, is documented by Mandel,[38] who discusses and compares two series of reading books for younger children, one the 'Rollo' series, popular in the nineteenth century, and the other the present day 'Dick and Jane' series:

> In the first group of books, the world is full of dangers and evil temptations, and the child himself is full of evil impulses that he must learn to control. In the second group, the world is full of good possibilities, and the child himself has only good impulses which should be given rein and encouragement. ... With all the potential for badness outside and inside Rollo, it is natural that he should be given some sort of mechanism to protect himself from danger. From the first, Rollo is being taught a code of Christian virtues which he is to adopt in order to resist the evil around and within him .... The first step in inculcating such a set of rules for behavior is to impress the child with the wisdom and sanctity of authority. Rollo himself must be taught to obey his parents unquestioningly. ... [39]
>
> While Rollo is adopting precepts, Dick is adapting to social experience ... Dick's world requires no constant watchfulness with confirmed inner virtues always on hand to protect him ... his world is distinct from the world of adults. Indeed adults foster the autonomy of Dick and his group. Each individual finds self-confirmation and a source of meaning in social interaction with his peers .... The children spend their time having fun while playing with one another, while going to school, or while participating in humorous little incidents described as funny or silly.[40]

Mandel's discussion sums up well the curricular implications of the endorsement by the school of particular models of the child, the adult, and the relationships that should exist between them, and it is particularly useful in that it takes its example from what is apparently the learning of a value neutral skill – how to read.

Models of the role of the teacher and of effective teaching will be adopted to accord with images of adult and child, and with preferred styles of relationships. But they will also depend on the value placed by society on teaching, which in turn will affect the type of person who becomes a teacher, and the experiences he is given to prepare him for the task. A view of effective teaching will also reflect the state of knowledge about technologies for implementing theoretical conceptions of the purposes of the curriculum. If effective teaching is extended to include planning as well as implementing the curriculum, then account must also be taken of what models are available for exemplifying a curriculum. In the last century, the curriculum could only be conceived as a schedule of content – facts to be learned or skills to be mastered, generally ranged under subject headings. Today we have discovered other possibilities: the curriculum can be seen in terms of aims and objectives, exploits or experiences, initiations or cultural confrontations. Also, broader definitions have been accepted for what can legitimately be part of a curriculum. Not only can 'subjects' appear in different forms, or be assimilated to one another in schemes of integration, but new areas of knowledge and experience, not before considered as material for a curriculum, can be imported – community service, black studies, making TV programmes, carrying out social and ecological surveys, to mention only some of the less extreme examples of innovation in curricular activities.

But, as has been pointed out, it is seldom the case that the choice of model is totally constrained by the total absence of alternatives. One of the factors which plays a large part in deciding which set of models will, in practice, be adopted is the nature of the school's input and output of students. Who are they, and where do they come from? Where will they go when they leave and what expectations will be held of them by those who will continue their education or give them employment? According to their family and community background, students will be more or less accepting of the school's valuation of what is suitable knowledge, more or less prepared to fit in with new definitions of proper social relationships, more or less ready to acquire new images of what they might become as adults. The extent to which the school accepts and encourages the inclinations of its entering students, or tries to change them, is largely a function of where they will go when they leave, and how far the new environments they will enter are capable of influencing the school. If the success of a secondary school is judged by the number of students it sends to universities and into prestigious occupations, then the demands of these institutions may outweigh the influence of the local community in determining where the school looks for appropriate models.

Moderating any interaction of pressures to adopt particular definitions of its task is the school's boundary – the psychological frontier that exists between the members of the organisation and their activities, and the outside world in the form of local and national communities and of institutions capable of influencing what the school does. Generally speaking, schools have strong boundaries, because inputs of resources into them are not directly linked to the sale of a product. The thought was well expressed by Edward Thring over a century ago:

> The old foundations [are] a great saving power in the land. Whatever their faults may be, they are generally free from meddling, free from the necessity of producing some show, something saleable. They are able to stand a storm without shrinking, and to face with calmness the morning letter-bag and the penny post.[41]

The worthy ambition of many a head teacher – 'to face with calmness the morning letter-bag' – is, as Thring perceptively observed, to be realised only if his output is not defined as 'saleable'. The desire to avoid commitment to a saleable output is one reason why schools strive to identify themselves with scholarly traditions and are reluctant to implement curricula which pursue overtly vocational objectives. However, schools are not always able to command this privileged position. At about the time that Thring was writing, English elementary schools were administered under a system of 'payment by results' which allowed them very little autonomy. But as well as boundary control which regulates the imposition of specific performance demands on the school, there may be control over the selection of students and teachers. It was commonly the case in the English secondary school that the entry of students could be limited to those most likely to import ideas, behaviours and aspirations consonant with the established 'theory' of the institution.

Since the school functions as a single organisation, and its ability to function depends on keeping dissonance and conflict within reasonable bounds, an overall determinant of the character of the curriculum is the way in which accommodation is achieved between technology, task group and theory. This can be best illustrated by examples. The English elementary school in the nineteenth century used a mass production technology, based on formal classrooms and simple teacher/pupil interaction with little use of technical aids to learning. The social system was paternal and authoritarian. Children were expected to follow instructions and to be in all ways subordinate to and respectful of the wishes of teachers who themselves were products of authoritarian and rule-bound training colleges. The theory of the task was that it was the job of the school to inculcate basic moral values, as propagated by the established church, and the basic skills of reading, writing and simple calculation. The three elements of theory, social system and technology were in harmony. It is difficult to see how a major shift could have taken place in any one of them without setting up an intolerable dissonance.

Formal methods reflected the commonly held definition of the task and of the nature of children. The established style of social relationships allowed that task to be carried out effectively. The modern primary school presents a balance of a different type. The technology is seen in much more interactive terms with liberal use of teaching aids – not necessarily in the form of film strips and tape-recorders, more often in the shape of scissors, paste and *papier mâché*. The social system tends to the maternal and the familial, while the theory construes children as active learners and teaching as an engagement in a humanistic activity which attends to basic skill requirements but also stresses, through concepts of growth, harmony and discovery, the need to foster the developing social and intellectual capacities of the child. Here too, the technology, social system and theory are consonant, but produce an arena for the enactment of curriculum that is supportive of quite different knowledge and values. Again, the whole would seem to be dependent on the harmony of the parts. The theory could not be implemented by the technology of the nineteenth century, nor could a nineteenth-century technology be sustained by the social system as it now exists.

Finally, the school will tend to reduce conflict between its methods of operation and the demands and constraints laid upon it by other institutions and by society at large. This is another aspect of the boundary question. Conflict can be reduced by conformity, but it can also be avoided by isolating the school, or some part of it, from outside forces. The latter response is less likely when demands are mediated through the inputs or outputs of students. These must cross the boundary, and control is difficult. When there was widespread selection for different types of secondary education at age eleven, primary schools had to shape their activities according to the pressures of the secondary sector. Internal and external consonance are mutually dependent. External forces that provide a means of establishing internal harmony will be acceded to. English primary schools in the 1960s were ready to accept new approaches to mathematics teaching which were being pressed by academics and HMIs because this provided them with the shift in technology that was needed to harmonise it with shifts in theory and in the social system. However, it is unlikely that schools will change their internal elements in ways that will result in severe disequilibrium with environmental forces. The cases where this does occur are exceptional. A recent example was that of the William Tyndale Junior School in London where severe curricular disagreements between staff, parents, managers and local authority led to an official enquiry and to dismissals, resignations and disciplinary proceedings.[42] The root of the problem was that the curriculum of the school, under the influence of a new head and deputy appointed from outside, had become far removed from the concept of a suitable curriculum held by many parents. The actual breakdown came through the special circumstance that, being in an area of urban depopulation and declining rolls, the school was unable to defend its boundaries and parents exercised their right to send their children to other schools in the neighbourhood.

Accounting for curriculum change

This elaboration of the few simple propositions with which we started provides an account of the stabilising tendencies which characterise the school as an organisation and tend to shape the form that the curriculum takes. But what account can it give of curriculum change? According to the view described, change comes about mainly as a result of change in the factors in the environment of the school that control the internal balance between technology, social system and theory. This does not provide an answer for the theorist who wants to know why any social change comes about, because it pushes that fundamental question one stage further back without trying to solve it. But for those with a practical interest in curriculum change it offers ways of conceptualising problems of change that can have some relevance to action. Schools are seen as reflections of particular sets of the stock of models of theorising, doing and relating that society possesses at any given time. The stock is continually changing. The range of models increases as new ones become popular, but at the same time old ones are discarded.[43] Which set of models is relevant for any particular school depends on the character of its inputs and outputs, and the degree to which it can in other respects control its boundaries so that it can respond selectively to the pressures and constraints of outside forces and institutions. These are matters which are to a large extent under administrative control. Local authorities, for example, determine what a school's catchment area for student recruitment shall be. The question of curriculum change is mainly a question about change in the technology of the school, using that word in the broad sense that was indicated earlier.[44] That is, it is mainly a process question. How does the school carry out its work? And why this way rather than that? But technology is inseparable from theory and social system. The answer to 'why this way?' is partly 'because that is how we see the task', and partly 'because we get along together better that way'. So changes in ways of seeing and ways of 'getting along' are linked with changes in the means by which the school gets its work done. An account of curriculum change in the English public school along these lines would point to different things than those highlighted by conflict theory: the change in the 'theory' of the gentleman held in the upper reaches of society from a Christian to a more secular one, which is reflected in a more familial and less monastic social system in the school. The ways in which public authorities have asserted more and more control over the school through legislation and imposition of financial regulation, and how the schools have resisted this erosion of their boundaries by devices such as the development of the relationship with preparatory schools to assure a homogeneous intake and the sedulous fostering of a mythology of the school and its products: 'When the editors [of the *Public Schools Year Book*, 1904] spoke about "public school spirit" and "public school men" they enveloped the public schools in an air of mystery in order to distinguish them from state supported institutions and isolate them from criticism';[45] and finally the changes in the university curriculum, which the schools have not been able to resist, and which has led to the development of strong commitments to science education.

Implications for planning

Whether this kind of account is a more satisfactory one than the kind suggested earlier in terms of a conflict interpretation all depends on the purposes of the theoriser. It is hard to see what consequences a conflict analysis can have for someone interested in planning a curriculum. It gives him the choice of being on the side of social evolution, or against it. Either way, his influence can only be to delay or to speed up processes over which he has no significant control. A functional perspective on change does leave room for the planner, though it also properly reminds him of the magnitude of his task. First of all there is no suggestion that the general course of events is predetermined, nor, in the nature of things, is there any one unique resolution of the dissonance problem. What such analysis does suggest is that planning that sees the curriculum simply in terms of a technology deployed by the school is likely to produce disappointing results, because, while many of the factors controlling the nature of the technology are open to managerial intervention, they are factors which are not usually thought of as belonging to the arena of curriculum decision-making – decisions on the supply and training of teachers, on the processes by which students are passed from one school to another, and by which they find their ways to employment and to higher education, on the nature of a school's catchment area and the kinds of control it should exercise over the admission of students. To recognise that the form of a curriculum is the result of shifting balances in complex systems, and to recognise also that many future states of the system are at any time possible is to deny any necessary connection between managerial decision and practical outcome. It is not, however, to deny a role to purposeful management. In fact, once we accept that management is not simply the act of bringing about pre-specified states of the system and implementing predetermined objectives, its role is enhanced. It is no longer a technical affair of matching means to ends, but a creative process depending on wide-ranging consultation, on the interactive consideration of ends and means and on the exercise of judgment over conflicts of interest. Its role is also enhanced in that we can no longer clearly distinguish between the managers and the managed. If management is not just technique, then it is not just a matter for the technical experts, but for all those who have knowledge of and perspectives on the system, and for all those who look to it to respond to their aims, wants and desires. To construe the system in other ways, to see it as a rationally planned delivery system, is to move away from rather than towards the realisation of the purposes the curriculum is intended to secure.[46] Effective curriculum management involves the clarification of purposes, the identification of possible system states that would contribute to the realisation of those purposes, and decisions on how and where to operate on the factors controlling curriculum stability to try to bring about the state chosen as most suitable. Many curriculum changes have in fact been introduced in this indirect way, though seldom as part of a deliberate and systematic overall policy. Changes in the curriculum of the English primary school were provoked by a policy of designing buildings of a type that would encourage the development of social systems supportive of the theory and technology of open class teaching. At the same time the likelihood that the new technology would be implemented was increased by the move to comprehensive intakes into secondary schools and the consequent freeing of the primary school from the need to prepare children for specific achievement tests at age 11. It may be argued that if curriculum change were to be regularly planned in this all-embracing manner, it would require the creation of authorities with undesirably broad powers. But if these powers are used in the service of purposes that are widely and democratically deliberated on, this would seem to be advantageous. It does not follow that because powers are wide they have to be used for the furtherance of unique and all-embracing solutions. If we see the curriculum as determined by environments that are usually in some sense 'local', rather than by national or global power struggles, then the management of the curriculum must be to a large degree local. It is surely better that powers should exist which can ensure the effective determination and pursuit of curricular purposes, rather than that authorities should have the ability to intervene in ways that upset the system without achieving any declared purpose. State legislation in the United States has been very effective in implementing accountability schemes, but this means of opening the boundary of the school has affected its technology in ways that conflict with theory and social system. There has been a consequent lowering of teacher morale and satisfaction without any solid achievement of purpose to compensate for this. The objective of creating possibilities for more comprehensive approaches to the management of the curriculum would be that systems could be coaxed towards desired ends, not that attempts could be made to force them in particular directions.

Seeing schools as systems that tend towards equilibrium leads to an emphasis on 'gradualism' in planning. The belief that change should be brought about rapidly or in revolutionary ways is rejected in favour of change strategies that allow that the interests of the community may best be served by moving in directions that are discovered rather than predetermined and by avoiding attempts to force the immediate realisation of stated goals. The notion is one of working towards desirable states of affairs, rather than for the achievement of highly specific objectives.[47] The gradualist would, for example, have argued in the 1960s against the idea that all English secondary schools should, at some early and predetermined point in time, become comprehensive (basically, to change the input to the schools). He would have pointed to the fact that different schools in different parts of the country were in varying degrees ready for such a change. In some places, reorganisation would strain the social system of the school by amalgamating buildings on widely separated sites, in others there would be dissonance with the values of the local community, in others technological problems in providing a curriculum because of a lack of suitable models and suitable teachers. This is not an argument in favour of a doctrinaire preservation of class inequalities, but in favour of seeing problem solution as something that, to be effective, must take account of local circumstances and match expectations to the power of institutions to bring about change. Our purposes are not served by tactics which risk breakdowns leading to a hardening of opposition to innovation (as in the William Tyndale case), nor by encouraging people to have unrealistic beliefs in the capacity of schools to solve deep-seated social problems. A slower approach may serve us better: the time gained can be used to ask and to answer questions about the curriculum which must otherwise be glossed over. In the case of the comprehensive schools, how, in terms of actual encounters between teachers, children and materials, are the new forms of organisation to be used as arenas for the pursuit of new aims and purposes? Merely to declare a school comprehensive, even to provide it with a nationally approved curriculum, is not enough.[48]

The argument about gradualism brings us full circle, for the question of whether we should incline to evolution or revolution relates closely to our theoretical views on whether, or to what extent, socio-cultural change moves in an inevitable direction, and whether we prefer a functionalist or a conflict interpretation of how change comes about. The position put forward here is that, although the distinction between function and conflict may in some ways be a spurious one, there is for practical purposes a real choice of perspective to be made, and one that we cannot avoid by adopting a 'managerial' stance towards curriculum planning: that, although any view of curriculum change is necessarily partial and incomplete, a functional view is theoretically satisfactory and allows us possibilities for developing theories of effective practice in the arena of curriculum planning. To hold the opposite view is to subscribe to a fundamentally pessimistic conception of the role of the planner, and to deny that curriculum theory can ever be anything other than a branch of social theory that concerns itself with the connections between curricular forms and the patterns of conflict between power groups in society. Like the arch conservative, the revolutionary already knows what the ends of action should be. Neither is prepared to have his view of reality disconfirmed. Subscription to the idea of evolution implies an openness towards the directions that change might take and a commitment to the discovery of those directions through processes of deliberation in which questions of public policy are decided in ways that respect the wishes of all those who will be affected by the answers which are given.

6 Rationalism or humanism? The future of Curriculum Studies

The problems of curriculum are also the problems of Curriculum Studies. In two senses. First, the justification for the existence of a field[1] calling itself Curriculum Studies is that it clarifies the nature of curriculum problems and the means by which they are solved. But second, and equally important, Curriculum Studies is, like curriculum itself, concerned with evaluating ways of knowing, with shaping attitudes towards knowledge and with creating contexts for the discussion and criticism of its own subject matter. If we believe that deliberation and judgment can be powerful instruments for the definition and solution of curriculum problems, then we must also have confidence that, through deliberation and judgment, Curriculum Studies can shape its own future. We are not compelled simply to wait and see where fashion, or political, social or technological developments take us. We can and should examine the futures that might exist for Curriculum Studies, and work to bring about a future that reflects the nature and needs of the field in so far as we can discover them. Especially should we do this at a time when, on the one hand, curriculum problems in the industrial West are beginning to assume an enhanced social and political importance and, on the other, the general breakdown of long-established academic values and traditions provides an arena in which all manner of transient enthusiasms can appear as solutions to the problems of academic disciplines in search of an identity. What futures might be attainable is a question I have chosen to examine in relation to a view of practical and theoretic activity that opposes 'rationalism' to 'humanism'. There are many more dimensions to the issue than this simple dichotomy would suggest: but the history of thought in the West over the last few centuries indicates it is an essential starting point, and the history of Curriculum Studies itself reveals it as a central consideration in deciding what kinds of intellectual commitments the field could or should make.

The choice of terminology is not easy. I am speaking here of currents

Table 2 *Contrasting features of rationalism and humanism*

Rationalism	*Humanism*
PREMISES	
Reductionist	Holistic
Materialist	Value oriented
'End of Ideology/Cult of the Fact'	Idealistic
Emphasis on 'givens'	Relevance of experience
Ahistorical	Historical
PROCEDURES	
Convergent	Divergent
Objective	Subjective
Empirical	Impressionistic
Quantitative	Qualitative
Experimental	Observational
Analytical	Interpretative
Demonstrative	Judgmental
TRUTH TESTS	
Prediction	Understanding
Replicability	Plausibility
'Significance'	Meaning
Fit with theory	Fit with argument
EMPHASES	
Means	Ends
Objectives	Intentions
Innovation	Development
Intervention	Nurturing
Mass phenomena	The individual
CHARACTERISTICS	
Scientific	Artistic/creative
Utilitarian	Romantic
Tough-minded	Tender-minded
Authoritarian	Permissive
Instrumental	Expressive
Naturalistic	Imaginative
Puritanical	Hedonistic
Efficient	Ethical
Directive	Interactive

of thought which are very broad and which have changed over time in a complex manner. The labels I have applied denote but do not describe: to oppose rationalism to humanism is not to suggest that humanism is irrational. Yet the basic opposition I have in mind has been clear in the fields of ideas, of research and of general culture. It is perhaps best brought out by listing some of the antithetical notions and procedures which may, in any given instance, characterise the one approach or the other (see Table 2). The list suggests the ramified nature of the two traditions, and also some of the possibilities that exist for bringing them closer together. Some terms which are here treated as subordinate obviously have claims on the role of label terms – 'artistic', 'romantic', 'empirical', 'scientific', 'utilitarian'. But the choice of any of these would be either limiting or misleading. Rationalism is not 'merely' empirical, and it is a commonplace that major achievements in science have depended on observation, interpretation and imagination. The case of science is important for the later argument. Like most, if not all, areas of disciplinary enquiry it does not, on an objective view, stand in either the rationalist or the humanist tradition. But the forging of links is not, and has not been, the order of the day. Rather the disciplines are competed over and annexed to one tradition or the other. Science is not necessarily of the rationalist camp, but it has been claimed for it and the claim, though hotly contested, has been widely seen as legitimate. This state of affairs has been remarked on many times:

> The *status quo* ... reveals a condition of marked cleavage, with rather dubious attempts here and there to throw temporary bridges across the chasm and thus secure an appearance of unity ... the division in thought lives on and reveals itself not alone in science, philosophy and religion, but in current social theory and in education.[2]

Like other areas of thought and endeavour, Curriculum Studies has had to accommodate itself to the rival pressures and attractions of these great intellectual traditions. Before it became organised as a field of study in universities and colleges its exponents leaned to the humanistic school. Influential statements about what should be taught or how learning should be organised due to theorists such as Rousseau, Herbart and Froebel dealt primarily in metaphors stressing observation, understanding and nurturing, though their ideas were also shaped by the English empiricist tradition stemming from Locke. The institutionalisation of Curriculum Studies saw its capture by the rationalists whose technological ambitions left it with a legacy of metaphors drawn from engineering, experimental psychology and scientific management.[3] But the claim on the field was not exclusive, and the humanistic approach still found powerful voices, notably, and for many years, that of Dewey. More recently there have been signs that, after a long reign, rationalism is suffering challenges that it is increasingly impotent to respond to, as much from a loss of self-confidence as from the strength of counter positions. Curriculum Studies may be about to undergo a phase change, perhaps a rapid one given the 'domino effects' which are likely to ensue when outward assaults are combined with a failure of morale. Scenarios of Marxian inevitability for the demise of 'rational' Curriculum Studies are beginning to be written. In Pinar's terminology, the long dominance of the 'traditionalist' is coming to an end, and the day of the purveyors of compromise, the 'conceptual empiricists', promises to be short. The future lies with the 'reconceptualists' who are already among us.[4] The intention or the interpretation may be exaggerated, but new positions are being taken up, and the lines are being drawn very largely in terms of the great coalitions of rationalism on the one side and humanism on the other.

We should note that Curriculum Studies is not alone in sensing the collapse of long-standing metaphors and paradigms, though it may feel the loss more acutely since its intellectual clothes were largely borrowed in the first place and its ability to fit itself out for new climates must therefore be open to some doubt. Movements away from rational strategies and metaphors are currently characteristic of many people-oriented disciplines, and also of some of the more popular currents of thought. In the social sciences Alfred Schutz has been rediscovered and Berger and Luckmann's *Social Construction of Reality* has become required reading. De-schoolers began probing the deficiencies of traditional approaches to public education at about the same time that new wave psychologists began to make their contribution to what has been christened the 'consciousness revolution'. Questioning of the epistemological bases of academic disciplines has echoed popular disillusionment with the qualities of life styles offered by a society dominated by technological authoritarianism.[5] The world is reconceived as a work of meaning and imagination at the very moment when Skinner and others proclaim the final end of ideology.[6] As the well-stocked shelves of the paperback book stores witness, Sartre's suggestion that 'the proper function of psychology is to improve the biography of the individual' is being enthusiastically embraced.

Yet, curiously, it was the so-called 'hard sciences' that were the first to produce findings that sapped at the foundations of naive materialism. Einstein showed that phenomena appear differently according to where you stand and how fast you are moving; Heisenberg enunciated the indeterminacy principle; light was declared to be both wave and particle. All of this happened over fifty years ago; now scientists talk happily of 'black holes' and 'anti-matter'. As a writer in the *Saturday Review* put it: 'Already it is impossible to distinguish statements by famous scientists from those by great mystics'.[7] The fallacy of the supreme communicability of scientific insights has had to be abandoned. After an unrewarding attempt to exchange ideas, Einstein wrote to Bohr: 'a man like you comes and one would expect that two like minded persons had met, yet we are unable to find a common language. Maybe we physicists ought to agree upon certain fundamentals ... before embarking on discussions.'[8] With hard science no longer accepting the role of superego, what limits to imagining can exist? If, as shown in a *New Scientist* poll, 67 per cent of scientists accept the reality or possibility of extra-sensory perception, why should Curriculum Studies baulk at concepts such as consciousness or transcendence? In the first flush of freedom at the relaxation of the grip of the rational and the scientific, many ill-assorted ideas find themselves in joyous coalition, clamouring to be heard.

Before trying to make sense of this situation from the point of view of Curriculum Studies, it is necessary to consider in more detail the traditions of rationalism and humanism that were introduced simply in terms of lists of epithets. What I refer to by the shorthand of 'rationalism' is the view that reality is objectively extant and that value-free methods of studying it can be found. Interest is essentially in the 'givens' of a situation, not in its prior history or in the personal views and experiences of those involved in it. 'Humanism', on the other hand, believes in the centrality of values, that 'to profess no politics, to believe in the end-of-ideology, is itself a political and an ideological act.'[9] It believes in the need to treat wholes rather than parts, and to give attention to the history of the situations studied and to the subjective reports of participants in them. It is prepared to trust qualitative judgment and is often inclined to prefer it to quantitative measurement. In education, the humanist is unimpressed by learning theories that regard knowledge as 'external to the knower, there to be discovered, mastered, learned',[10] preferring to believe that 'the student will only be in a position to learn when he is committed to act upon his world' and that 'The desire to create meanings is not satisfied by the authoritarian confrontation of student with knowledge structures, no matter how teachable.'[11]

But apart from basic premises about the nature of knowledge, certain emphases tend to be associated with rationalist and humanist modes of thought which, on a logical view, may not seem to be definitely inherent in them. Rationalism stresses means rather than ends, objectives rather than intentions, and inclines to innovation and to intervention where humanism favours development and nurturing. The rational mode is scientific, technological and utilitarian, where the humanistic is romantic, artistic and creative. To what extent is the acceptance of secondary characteristics such as these a necessary consequence of adopting one of the basic modes? For example, can the rational mode handle ends other than in the form of preset objectives? Does the concept of 'affective' objectives offer something of a different order from the 'cognitive'?[12] If 'appreciation of literature is set as an affective aim, we beg the question, "Appreciation of it as what?" ' If the idea is that it be appreciated as an artefact, the aim falls short of the humanist aspiration. (Here we might usefully note Greene's distinction between, on the one hand, the British and the American traditions of literary criticism that treat works as artefacts and, on the other, the Continental tradition that interests itself in the subjective understanding of the reader – the critic as 'critic of consciousness'.) To introduce the affective objective is merely to perpetuate the heresy that to correct for what objective empiricism leaves out you must create a reserve area – J. S. Mill's 'culture of the feelings' – where you look after that something. According to this view, the mind is one thing and thinks and decides and takes action: the feelings are another and must be tended. Art and literature serve this purpose and are therefore necessary to keep the technocrat civilised.[13]

One of the most difficult problems in understanding the nature of rationalism and humanism is to decide how far and in what ways their differing characters relate to their subject matters and methods of truth seeking, and how far to social causes. The interaction of ideas and social structures has given to the humanist/rationalist polarity different aspects at different epochs and in different places, but it is traceable from the earliest times. Objective, reductionist philosophies, such as those of Empedocles and Epicurus, had little in common with the humanism of Socrates and Aristotle. But in classical thought humanism was the dominant theme. The full force of the rational approach had to await the development of instruments of data collection sufficiently precise and powerful to lift objectivist ideas out of the realm of metaphysical speculation. To that point it was the humanist who enjoyed the advantage of access to data. With Kepler, Galileo and Copernicus, objectivist speculation gives way to objectivist observation and measurement, and soon the priority of facts over theories became an established doctrine. Descartes carried the process further and effected the total separation of matter from mind and facts from ideas.

> In Bacon and Descartes, for the first time, ... the tradition of linguistic and literary studies which had constituted the bases of the humanities in the Renaissance comes into sharp conflict with the claims of natural philosophy to the possession both of a superior method of enquiry and of superior possibilities of utility to man.[14]

With the growth of universities, ideas became increasingly institutionalised, and ways of thinking took on the appearance of cultures rather than philosophical systems. At the same time, technological innovation gave a new twist to the career of scientific rationalism as a social force. Snow maintains that the two cultures have now grown completely apart. The focus of the polarity that he emphasises is between 'scientists' and 'literary intellectuals'. The clashing point of the two cultures should, he says, 'produce creative chances ... the chances are there now. But they are there, as it were, in a vacuum, because those in the two cultures can't talk to each other.' Describing his own experience, he says:

> constantly I felt I was moving among two groups – comparable in intelligence, identical in race, not grossly different in social origin, earning about the same income, who had almost ceased to communicate at all, who in intellectual, moral and psychological climate had so little in common that instead of going from Burlington House or South Kensington to Chelsea, one might have crossed the ocean.

But perhaps this is a particularly English problem, caused by a highly specialised educational system? Snow thinks not:

> one found Greenwich Village talking precisely the same language as Chelsea, and both having about as much communication with MIT as though the scientists spoke nothing but Tibetan. For this is not just our problem ... this is the problem of the entire West.[15]

The problem of how ways of knowing relate to the development of cultures is something that Curriculum Studies should interest itself in far more than it has. A number of studies have shown that, to a very important degree, learning is a way of mediating and controlling some aspects of the personal environment, and that different styles of learning associated with different academic disciplines serve this function, depending on the personality of particular individuals. Positive feedback from experience in a discipline leads to a progressive focussing of commitment and, conversely, individuals whose personalities do not 'fit' are discouraged by the styles of thinking, teaching, learning and assessment they encounter.[16] Hudson makes a similar point:

> It is assumptions, prejudices and implicit metaphors that are the true burden of what passes between teacher and taught. Facts, skills, details are in comparison ephemeral, in the sciences especially, but in the arts as well. They are also identifiable – and rejectable. What the teacher spells out, the pupil can question. What he assumes, especially from a position of unchallenged legitimacy, his pupils will tend to swallow whole and unawares.[17]
>
> It may be that a single system of values embraces the individual's perceptions of academic institutions; his perceptions of himself; and his demonstrable behavior. That the opposition between authority and freedom, self expression and self control, and masculinity and femininity are among the basic conflicts around which an individual's mental life develops.[18]

If adherence to particular disciplines is often, if not always, associated with particular and coherent styles of controlling the personal environment, it is to be expected that exponents of curriculum theory based on a view of knowledge as external to the knower will be in an adversary position towards those who prefer to see knowledge acquisition as the act of creating personal meanings.

Types of 'truth strategy'

But, while psycho-social forces may hold the key to the ultimate divorce of the rational and the human, the origin of the separation – the reason why that major cleavage and not some other should be institutionalised – must lie in some necessary epistemological distinction between them. A suggestive model to consider here is that of Thompson.[19] If disciplines achieve a social existence, it is because they set out to answer questions that depend for their correct formulation and solution on the use of particular and limited strategies of truth seeking. Thompson suggests that the determining factors underlying these strategies can be described by reference to two basic dimensions representing: (i) the extent to which formulating and answering questions depends on experience of the real world, and (ii) the extent to which the subject matter of the discipline is capable of being codified. A simple dichotomy on these dimensions, when set orthogonally to each other, yields four truth strategies (Figure 3): (i) the Scientific, which depends on data and has ample resources for codifying; (ii) the Direct, which also is data dependent, but has only limited possibilities for codifying; (iii) the Analytic, which is not data dependent because it creates its own axioms, but having created them can treat them in a highly codified manner; and (iv) the Inspirational, which is not reliant on data and deals in systems of thinking that do not lend themselves to codification. (Judgment about whether this is indeed the case may be relative rather than absolute. In the example from archaeology quoted later, the writer being criticised for 'inspirationalism' had based his theorising on some 'hard' data, though his ideas had previously been put forward by people with less concern for facts.) Scientific truth strategies are employed in, for example, physics, while history would be an instance of a discipline with a direct strategy. Mathematics and symbolic logic are disciplines that use an analytic strategy. The inspirational strategy is harder to identify with the established disciplines, because becoming established involves being or claiming to be something more than 'merely' inspirational. But elements of the inspirational are to be in many areas of thought, not least in Curriculum Studies, the subject matter of which invites the creation of utopian scenarios which are not formulated according to any demonstrable logic, and which do not have any substantial foundation in data.[20] In fact, although type cases exist, most areas of academic endeavour are to some extent hybrid in respect of the truth strategies they deploy, and most have, over time, been subjected to shifting emphases on their relative importance. A final point to note is that each strategy has its appropriate kind of truth test. Scientific theories have to show that they are consistent with theory that is already accepted, in direct disciplines theories are evaluated through informed debate, analytical theories (theorems) are shown to be correct or incorrect by reference to the logic of the system and inspirational theories depend for their acceptance on the personal authority of their proposers.

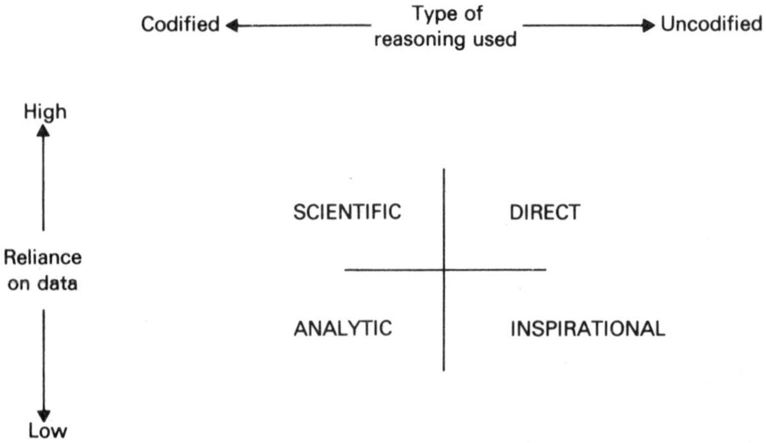

Figure 3 Four 'truth strategies' (after J. D. Thompson *et al.*, 'Truth strategies and university organisation', *Educational Administration Quarterly*, 5, 1969, pp. 4–25)

Though the Truth Strategies model shows up the argument over rationalist and humanistic orientations as being more than just a matter of contention over antithetical positions, it can still be criticised for being over simple. The way it is constructed tends to imply an emphasis on categorising truth strategies according to the extent to which their application will produce conclusions that command widespread assent because they can be demonstrated from the application of rules or the analysis of data. Curriculum, it could be justly claimed, is an area where agreement is not the issue. It is rather an area of 'contested concepts',[21] one of those humane studies which are 'most alive when they ... look for devices of explanation and appreciation that will enable them to preserve as much as possible of the variety, the uniqueness, the unexpectedness, the complexity, the originality, that distinguish what men are capable of doing at their best from what they must do, or tend generally to do, as biological organisms or members of a community', as opposed to the sciences which are 'most successful when they seek to move from the diversity and particularity of their observations towards as high a degree of unity, uniformity, simplicity and necessity as their materials permit'.[22] The criticism is allowed, but we need not be seriously concerned by it if our intention is simply to use the model to understand better some of the considerations which should be taken into account in a discussion of possible futures for Curriculum Studies and not to propose an all-embracing explanation of disciplinary activity.

Application of the model suggests that our views on the directions which Curriculum Studies might take will depend on the degree to which, and the ways in which, we see it as being concerned with data. To move away from 'scientific' strategies is not necessarily to reject the idea that we should be centrally concerned with gathering, interpreting and evaluating data. Direct strategies of truth seeking – history is the best example – while they do not attempt to apply rationalistic modes of enquiry to the phenomena they study, are nevertheless data based. Could Curriculum Studies be 'reconceived' and yet remain data based, rather than become a study focussed on 'grand theory' or on intuitions, as seems to be implied in some 'reconceptualist' writings? A consideration of the kinds of data with which Curriculum Studies deals suggests that they should be handled in ways appropriate to a humane discipline with a direct strategy. Data on classrooms, on learning, on the activities of designing and evaluating curricula are patently not to be compared to the data of the natural sciences. The experience to which Curriculum Studies must attend is to a degree anecdotal in the way that the experience of interest to historians is anecdotal; to a degree it is apprehended in the form of impressions rather than discrete facts. Sometimes it can lend itself to more systematic codification, and sometimes to theorising at the level of simple model building, but always the data relate to open systems where control of variables is an artificial procedure and always the phenomena under study are liable to change as educational systems change and as society itself changes. Nowhere can we point to data that are inherently codifiable to the extent that they could support a scientific strategy involving replicability and demonstrations of consistency with already validated explanatory theory. Any attempt to set up measurable and stable variables compels the enquiry to fit the measurement system rather than allowing it to address the substantive questions of the field,[23] and leads with greater or lesser certainty to irrelevance and triviality.[24]

The argument in Curriculum Studies has not, in fact, been about how far it can expand into the area of 'true science', but rather how far it should associate itself with attempts by other non-science disciplines, such as psychology and sociology, to declare themselves 'scientific' – that is, to attempt to shift the boundary of the scientific strategy rather than find ways in which their central concerns could be effectively dealt with through a truly scientific mode of enquiry. This they do, not because of the nature of the phenomena to be studied, but for sociological reasons. The scientific strategy enjoys high prestige, and quasi adoption of its procedures promises high status and ready funding for research. There is also the seductive prospect of setting up forms of research which are cumulative in their results; but if the field is not fitted for the strategy, all that results is an accumulation of irrelevance. In their adoption of scientific methodology, students of human behaviour have shown the zeal of the convert – they are more catholic than the Pope, and, for good measure, have modelled themselves on a Victorian conception of science that scientists themselves have long abandoned.

Ways ahead

The phase of institutionalisation of enquiries in education, especially in the USA, was marked by a tendency to call in the 'scientific manager' and later the 'behavioral scientist' as a kind of colonist and allow him a mandate over the field. Politically, this move was understandable at a time when belief was widespread that research into human affairs could and should be scientific – far better colonial status under a well-connected regime than academic oblivion. But, as the strength and reputation of the occupying power wanes, how should Curriculum Studies respond? Four possible lines of development seem worth considering, if it is agreed that the object of study is to provide a theoretic understanding of actual events or practical means of improving our control over them:

(i) the adoption of a purely eclectic approach, making use of whatever policies or procedures seem worthwhile on any given occasion;
(ii) the search for a way of conceptualising a middle ground that is data based, but is neither art nor science;
(iii) the exchange of colonisation by disciplines using scientific strategies for colonisation by those that deploy direct ones – Art, Literature, History;
(iv) the creation of a direct strategy particular to Curriculum Studies.

The eclectic approach is the one that secures adoption by default. It could justly be said that, in spite of the predominance of rational paradigms, Curriculum Studies already is an eclectic field, and this can be claimed as a very proper approach for any enquiry concerned with practical human problems. No doubt there is a sense in which the field always will be eclectic, whether consciously or not. But there are significant drawbacks in the deliberate encouragement of eclecticism. To disown the possibility that it could have any special expertise of its own, or, worse, to suggest that the problems it concerns itself with do not need any particular expertise for their solution, is to create a situation in which Curriculum Studies is unlikely to attract substantial support in the community. More important, in terms of the kinds of arguments about the nature of knowledge and enquiry that we have been concerned with, is the consideration that, while Curriculum Studies may occupy an uncertain position in terms of the rationalist/humanist polarity it does have its own central problems and it does deal in data that lend themselves to only a certain limited range of truth strategies. To opt for eclecticism is to deny the central business of the field, and of any field or discipline, which is to clarify the nature of its core problems, however hard an enterprise that may be.

The 'middle ground' solution leads to other kinds of difficulties. It is certainly a legitimate way of seeking for Curriculum Studies an intellectual identity and of confronting the inadequacies of rationalistic theorising without rushing to an opposite extreme. Moreover, promising beginnings of new conceptualisations lie at hand to be taken up – Simon's notion of 'sciences of the artificial',[25] systems theory in its various aspects,[26] Kelly's philosophy of constructive alternativism[27] – while older suggestions for integrative principles may yet prove to have scope for development – Spencer's evolutionary theories,[28] the pragmatism and the radical empiricism of Dewey and James.[29] But to embark on such an enterprise is to identify the solution before identifying the problem it is supposed to solve. Part of the reason for the crisis of Curriculum Studies is the placing of more emphasis on theory building than on the facts and events that the theories are supposed to explain or to allow control over. Accommodating the rational to the humanistic is an activity that has implications for Curriculum Studies but it is not one that the field itself is well placed to undertake, nor is it one that guarantees that priority will be accorded to the task which demands it – the identification and study of specifically curricular questions.

More immediately attractive is the idea that connections with behavioural science should be exchanged for collaboration with the established humanities. This would be to accept some of the implications of the trend to 'reconceptualisation'[30] that is already manifesting itself, and also to move in a direction that seems in tune with the general intellectual climate. The signs are already present that such an invasion of Curriculum Studies is a far from remote possibility. Literary criticism has been strongly advocated as a tool for curriculum evaluation,[31] aesthetics as a way of appreciating the experience of classrooms,[32] history as a way of understanding curriculum change[33] and drama as a leading metaphor for representing curriculum processes generally.[34] But this trend, if encouraged to the extent of becoming more than a catalyst for the development of ideas specific to the subject matter of Curriculum Studies, would perpetuate the unfortunate tradition that it is a parasitic field with no truth strategy that is uniquely its own. Though the humanities may seem to be more open than more rationally based disciplines to adaptation and accommodation, experience suggests that while colonising disciplines can often find a place in another field, they less easily become part of it but remain, essentially, concerned with the problems and procedures proper to their own area of enquiry. In a sense there may be a more serious problem in inviting humane studies into the curriculum field because, as the Truth Strategies model suggests, and as has been commonly argued, what is distinctive about the humanities is that each discipline is unique and not to be compared to its fellows, unlike the sciences which can be seen as more or less successful in the pursuit of a single strategy of enquiry.[35] What interests the historian or the literary critic is not just quantitatively but qualitatively different from what interests the student of curriculum.

A humanistic discipline of curriculum

This point can be used to positive effect in arguing for the last of the four possibilities listed earlier – the creation of a direct strategy particular to Curriculum Studies. If uniqueness is the hallmark of humane disciplines, and it is this type of truth seeking that is appropriate to the field, why should we think in terms other than the creation of a humanistic discipline of Curriculum? To do so would not deny the contribution that other disciplines might make. Each direct strategy can incorporate its own appropriate elements of the inspirational, the scientific or, more rarely, the axiomatic approach. A good example is afforded by archaeology. The central question around which its enquiries are based is, 'How did people live in times and places when there was little or no possibility of an historical record of their activities being preserved, and what was the nature of their culture and society?' The reconstruction of situations of which we have only limited artefactual evidence, supported by whatever sciences such as geology or climatology can add, is essentially a humanistic activity, and for long archaeology was seen exclusively in this light. But more recently it has been recognised that at least some of the data with which it is concerned can be analysed within the scientific mode, and always, of course, in a study where there are irreparable gaps in the available data, inspiration has an important part to play. It is kept in its place by the widely shared critical tradition that archaeologists have built up, and is not allowed to take charge of the direction of theorising. But, while some 'inspiration' remains excluded from serious research and discussion, other ideas which start out as inspirational become accepted.[36]

So, might the appropriate response of Curriculum Studies to the erosion of confidence in accepted modes of enquiry be to develop its own humanistic strategy with its own critical tradition? Could this answer the fundamental problems of the field and also be an undertaking reasonably within the bounds of achievement? In considering this we first have to note an apparent difference between Curriculum Studies as currently conceived and History, Art or Literature. It is concerned with an area of public policy making, and therefore with what should be done, as well as what is being done or what was done in the past. How much importance one attaches to this depends on one's prior commitment to a disciplinary position. As long as Curriculum Studies was dominated by aspirations to modes of enquiry stemming from rationalist traditions, the problem of distinguishing the descriptive from the prescriptive was felt as acute. But within a humane perspective it ceases to be a problem in the same way. Whatever use they make of data, the humanities are basically and inevitably about making value judgments:

> The humanities ... have been in the modern period, no less than for the Romans, means to the realization of some ideal or use over and above the understanding and appreciation of the peculiarly human achievements in art or philosophy or science which have been their subject matter. ... [I]f they are to retain their distinctive character and to be capable of constituting a peculiarly humanistic subject matter (the humanistic arts) must not be merely factual or descriptive but normative ... although they must also make use of the factual results about texts, sources and influences afforded by scholarly inquiry.[37]

In just this way Curriculum Studies must be concerned both with what is and with what might be. To try to separate the two and make them logically and procedurally distinct is to deprive it of any chance of coherent and useful development. Practical decisions must be based on judgments about facts, not on facts themselves, and, equally, objective study of curricula must include study of opinions, wants and values. Pursuit of a humanistic strategy of enquiry makes this not only possible but necessary. Because the humanities are concerned with making judgments on values as well as facts, their products inevitably have consequences for practical action. It happens in the case of curriculum that this action is decided on in an important and visible area of public policy-making while in the case of History, Art or Literature the connections with decision-making are less easy to see. But it is here that distinction needs to be made. Not between description and prescription within a discipline, but between disciplinary activity and the roles of responsible decision makers outside it. Though rationalists are very concerned about the first problem, they are less inclined to observe the logical and political gap between creating understandings and making decisions. The rationalist likes making decisions because he thinks he knows the answers. Rational theories of curriculum design tend to have strong authoritarian undertones. Curriculum 'reconceptualists' may also be interested in influencing what is taught because they are caught up in an intellectual movement that believes society should be changed and that change can come about only as the result of action. But 'action' is beginning to take on a new connotation, and to be distinguished from 'activism':

> The political activists have had their day. ... Neither lawful procedures nor politics-and-power can succeed against the Corporate State. ... The new generation, by experimenting with action at the level of consciousness, has shown the way to the one method of change that will work in today's post-industrial society.[38]

In such a climate, the neo-humanist may be content with a strategy for Curriculum Studies that places less emphasis on the theorist and researcher as decision-makers, and more on the necessity of incorporating value orientations in their own work.

The function of a humane study is to explain, interpret and evaluate a specific type of human activity and achievement in terms of the principles by which it is given meaning, significance and value. To do this it studies the phenomena of the activity which is its subject matter. In the case of curriculum:

> all those activities and enterprises in which curricula are planned, created, adopted, presented, experienced, criticised, attacked, defended and evaluated, as well as the objects which may be part of a curriculum, such as textbooks, apparatus and equipment, schedules, teachers guides, and so on ... [also] the plans, intentions, hopes, fears, dreams and the like of agents such as teachers, students, and curriculum developers or policy-makers.[39]

The purpose of studying these phenomena is to suggest answers to the peculiar questions with which the theorist and practitioner in the field are concerned: (i) In what ways are curriculum problems unique problems, and in what ways are they related to other classes of problems? (ii) What kinds of data and procedures are needed to define, elucidate and solve curriculum problems? (iii) How are judgments to be made about the adequacy of problem solutions and the procedures that led to them? (iv) How is the general context of ends and purposes created within which curriculum problems arise and within which they are solved and the adequacy of their solution judged? These are questions which can only be considered by reference to some conception of how and for what purposes the activity should be conducted. Normative concepts lead us to the kinds of data to which attention should be paid, and the understandings to which these give rise produce, in their turn, new normative contexts for curriculum tasks. There is no final answer to curriculum questions or to curriculum problems, but the answers given at any particular time must be tested within a critical tradition which the discipline creates for itself. The contributions that can be made to Curriculum Studies by other disciplines must be assessed by the criteria of the same critical tradition. If choice can be exercised, then the creation of a humane discipline of Curriculum Studies would seem to be the future that should be sought by those having either a theoretical or practical interest in the solution of curriculum problems.

Notes

Chapter 1 Introduction: Curriculum debates and curriculum studies

1 I. Illich, *Limits to Medicine: Medical Nemesis: The Expropriation of Health*, Harmondsworth, Penguin, 1977, p. 251.

2 The word 'intelligence' is used rather than 'data' or 'information' in acknowledgment of the fact that what we can know is neither precise nor totally trustworthy. But it is none the less essential to the formulation of public policy.

3 See Chapter 4.

4 Notably J. J. Schwab. See, for example, his 'The practical: a language for curriculum', *School Review*, 78, 1969, pp. 1–24.

5 The term is borrowed from John Holt (*How Children Fail*, New York, Pitman, 1964). It seems to be equally applicable to the behaviour of many educational policy-makers.

6 *Times Educational Supplement*, 15 October 1976, pp. 2–3, 'Has something gone wrong? How is it to be put right?'

7 Ibid., p. 2.

8 Loc. cit.

9 Loc. cit.

10 Incidentally, the remarks quoted and others like them in the paper are very theory laden. All kinds of positions of a very controversial kind on the nature and purpose of schools and on the nature of teaching and learning are taken up in the paper without any acknowledgment of their theoretical status and the way they prejudge questions of what the problems are or where solutions are to be sought.

11 It may be that the only available published version of the text is so incomplete that it gives a false impression of *non sequitur* in the argument. It should also be said that the passages quoted from this and subsequent 'debate' documents are from the sections directly related to curriculum questions. They may be very sound on other issues, such as the training of teachers.

12 Department of Education and Science, *Educating our Children: Four Subjects for Debate* (background paper for regional conferences, February and March 1977).

13 Ibid., p. 1.

14 Department of Education and Science and Welsh Office, 'Schools in England and Wales, current issues: an annotated agenda for discussion', November 1976.
15 Ibid., p. 1.
16 Ibid., p. 4.
17 Loc. cit.
18 Department of Education and Science, op. cit., p. 3.
19 Loc. cit.
20 Ibid., p. 4.
21 'Annotated agenda', pp. 4–5.
22 *Educating our Children*, p. 6.
23 Quoted in *Times Educational Supplement*, 3 December 1976, p. 12, 'Sniped at now from all sides'.
24 In particular the proponents of a 'return to basics' seized on a published study which they interpreted as showing that 'traditional' teaching styles achieved 'better' results than 'progressive styles' (N. Bennett *et al.*, *Teaching Styles and Pupil Progress*, London, Open Books, 1976).
25 *Education in Schools: A Consultative Document*, Cmnd 6869. London, HMSO, 1977.
26 Ibid., p. 11.
27 Ibid., p. 12.
28 10th Report from the Expenditure Committee, Session 1975/6, *Policy Making in the DES*, London, HMSO, 1976. Quoted in *Times Educational Supplement*, 1 October 1976, p. 17, 'Too secretive and too slow to give a lead'.
29 For a discussion and some references, see Chapter 5, pp. 70–2.
30 Papers 1–3, edited by C. B. Cox and A. E. Dyson, London, Critical Quarterly Society, 1969–70. Further issues appeared in 1975 and 1977 (C. B. Cox and R. Boyson (eds), *Black Paper, 1975: the Fight for Education*, London, Dent, and *Black Paper 1977*, London, Temple Smith).
31 D. A. Schon, *Beyond the Stable State: Public and Private Learning in a Changing Society*, London, Temple Smith, 1971, pp. 28–9.
32 Ibid., p. 29.
33 Ibid., p. 28.
34 See, for example, M. W. Apple, 'Ivan Illich and deschooling society: the politics of slogan systems', in M. Young and G. Whitty (eds), *Society, State and Schooling*, Ringmer, Falmer Press, 1977, pp. 93–121.
35 S. Frith and P. Corrigan, 'The politics of education', in ibid., p. 265.
36 J. Gretton and M. Jackson, *William Tyndale: Collapse of a School – or a System?*, London, Allen & Unwin, 1976, p. 49. Compare Leila Berg's account of an attempt to introduce non-authoritarian relationships between teachers and pupils by the headmaster of Risinghill School: 'some of the most rigid authoritarians, the most bitter opponents of Mr. Duane, were Communists. ... For these particular Communists, as for the most backward-looking Tory, people were tools, a means to an end, never individuals with a private worth' (L. Berg, *Risinghill: Death of a comprehensive school*, Harmondsworth, Penguin, 1968).
37 Schon, op. cit., Chapter 7.

Chapter 2 Thinking about the practical

1 For arguments in favour of such a division, see M. Johnson, 'The translation of curriculum into instruction', *Journal of Curriculum Studies*, 1, 1969, pp 115–31.

2 E. Thring, *Education and School*, Cambridge, Macmillan, 1864, p. 31.

3 For a discussion of the moral nature of curriculum decisions, see Chapter 4.

4 Friedrich Schelling, quoted in J. Habermas, 'Knowledge and interest', in D. Emmet and A. MacIntyre (eds), *Sociological Theory and Philosophical Analysis*, London, Macmillan, 1970, p. 37.

5 J. J. Schwab, 'The practical: a language for curriculum', *School Review*, 78, 1969, p. 3.

6 M. D. Shipman, *Inside a Curriculum Project: A case study in the process of curriculum change*, London, Methuen, 1974, p. 28.

7 Henri Poincaré, quoted in C. C. Gillispie, *The Edge of Objectivity: an Essay in the History of Scientific Ideas*, Princeton University Press, 1960, p. 155.

8 For a discussion of 'logic in use' and 'reconstructed logic', see A. Kaplan, *The Conduct of Inquiry: Methodology for Behavioral Science*, San Francisco, Chandler, 1964, p. 11.

9 In conducting a 'thought experiment' the scientist tries to imagine what would be the results of the occurrence of some state of affairs which could not be brought about in the laboratory. This may lead him to ideas or hypotheses which can be made the subject of controlled experiments. 'Thought experiments' in education tend to work the other way round. Rather than predicting the end results of action they assume desirable ends and prescribe the actions which, it is thought, will bring them about.

10 For an example of the consequences of the failure of inspirationalists to define the elements of their theories, see L. M. Smith and P. M. Keith, *Anatomy of Educational Innovation: An Organisational Analysis of an Elementary School*, New York, Wiley, 1971.

11 See, for example, D. F. Walker, 'Curriculum development in an art project' in W. A. Reid and D. F. Walker (eds), *Case Studies in Curriculum Change: Great Britain and the United States*, London, Routledge & Kegan Paul, 1975, pp. 91–135.

12 As McKinney and Westbury put it: the curriculum is 'an *idea* that becomes a thing' and 'development and renewal are only meaningful notions in so much as they are embedded in structures' (W. L. McKinney and I. Westbury, 'Stability and change; the public schools of Gary, Indiana, 1940–70' in Reid and Walker, op. cit., pp. 6 and 50).

13 A. Schutz, 'Concept and theory formation in the social sciences' in Emmet and MacIntyre, op cit., p. 2.

14 The methodology of curriculum research has been heavily influenced by these same considerations. See Chapter 3, p. 26 and compare Chapter 6, p. 103.

15 David Hume, *Treatise of Human Nature*, 2 vols, London, Dent, 1911 (reprinted, 1956).

16 K. R. Popper, *Objective Knowledge: An Evolutionary Approach*, Oxford University Press, 1972, p. 95.
17 Ibid., pp. 356–7.
18 See, for example, P. B. Medawar, *The Art of the Soluble*, London, Methuen, 1967.
19 K. Thompson and J. White, *Curriculum Development, A Dialogue*, London, Pitman, 1975. p. 13.
20 K. R. Popper, *Unended Quest: An Intellectual Autobiography*, Glasgow, Fontana, 1976, p. 133.
21 Ibid., p. 168.
22 D. A. Schon, *The Displacement of Concepts*, London, Tavistock, 1963, p. 176. For a fuller quotation, see Chapter 5, p. 84. A practical example of the vision-based theory of knowledge used in curriculum discussion is to be found in *The Sixth Form of the Future*, London, Headmasters' Association, 1968, *passim*.
23 Popper, op. cit., 1972, p. 71
24 M. Polanyi, *The Tacit Dimension*, New York, Doubleday, 1966, p. xi.
25 Popper, op. cit., 1972, pp. 260–1.
26 Ibid., p. 164.

Chapter 3 The concept of curriculum research

1 For discussion of the treatment of policy issues of this type, see G. Vickers, *The Art of Judgment*, London, Chapman & Hall, 1965 and D. McKie, *A Sadly Mismanaged Affair: A Political History of the Third London Airport*, London, Croom Helm, 1973.
2 F. N. Kerlinger, *Foundations of Behavioral Research*, New York, Holt, Rinehart, 1964. For a consideration of the position of Kerlinger and other psychometrically oriented educational researchers, see D. Hamilton, 'Some contrasting assumptions about case study research and survey analysis', Centre for Applied Research in Education, University of East Anglia, mimeo., 1976.
3 D. F. Walker, 'What curriculum research?', *Journal of Curriculum Studies*, 5, 1973, pp. 58–72.
4 For an extended treatment of the notion of the 'artifical', see H. A. Simon, *The Sciences of the Artificial*, Cambridge, Mass., MIT Press, 1969.
5 I. Scheffler, 'Is education a discipline?' in *Reason and Teaching*, London, Routledge & Kegan Paul, 1973, pp. 45–57.
6 Ibid., pp. 55–6.
7 Ibid., pp. 58–9.
8 To avoid a long digression at this point, the situation has been oversimplified. What is at issue is not so much whether curriculum research should or should not be 'scientific' as the question of what it means to be 'scientific'. Support for 'scientific' methods often turns out to be support for a reconstructed and fallacious logic of science (see also Chapter 2, note 8).
9 I. Westbury and W. Steimer, 'Curriculum: a discipline in search of its problems', *School Review*, 79, 1971, p. 262.

10 Franklin Bobbitt, *The Curriculum*, Boston, Houghton Mifflin, 1918 and *How to Make a Curriculum*, Boston, Houghton Mifflin, 1924. Though Bobbitt's theoretical prescriptions seem not unreasonable, the researches they inspired tended to degenerate into the trivial and the faintly ridiculous. Bobbitt's own *Curriculum Investigations* (University of Chicago Press, 1926) reports studies such as counts of topics treated in 180 issues of the *New York Times* and offers remarkable observations resulting from textual analysis of which the following may serve as an instance: 'A few passages were found which a reader could not interpret properly without a knowledge of the tables. The following sentence is an example: "No one can work twenty-four hours a day." The meaning of this sentence would not be clear to anyone who does not know the number of hours in a day' (p. 133).

11 The ideas of Bobbitt and of contemporaries such as Charters and Rugg were influential in securing important reforms of the curriculum in many American school districts. See H. L. Caswell, 'Emergence of the curriculum as a field of professional work and study', in H. F. Robison (ed.), *Precedents and Promise in the Curriculum Field*, New York, Teachers' College Press, 1966, pp. 1–11.

12 The bibliography of references to writers of the 'planning by objectives' school is extensive and well known and need not be repeated here. Whatever its shortcomings, this way in to curriculum design did provide a starting point for curriculum planners in the 1960s who were charged with producing major innovations and who looked in vain for alternative prescriptions.

13 See, for example, D. Hamilton, *Curriculum Evaluation*, London, Open Books, 1976, or D. Tawney (ed.), *Curriculum Evaluation Today: Trends and Implications*, London, Macmillan, 1976.

14 A reviewer of H. J. Butcher and H. B. Pont (eds), *Educational Research in Britain – 2* (University of London Press, 1970), comments on the 'lack of recognition that specific problems in one area have many similarities with those elsewhere. For instance, work on training medical students is not seen to have much in common with university teaching methods in general and workers in both these areas seem unaware of the more efficiency conscious and imaginative work in the field of management studies. ... Yet everyone is asking but not attempting to answer the same fundamental questions: "How do we learn, how do we decide what to learn and teach and by what criteria should we judge the results?" ' (*British Journal of Educational Psychology*, 42, 1972, p. 92). A commentator on the American scene comes to much the same conclusions: 'the characteristics of research methodology, which by convention and past practice have now acquired a high status in the field of educational research, act as a restriction on the study of significant problems in education' (S. K. Mitra, 'A brief note on American educational research,' *American Educational Research Journal*, 11, 1974, p. 43).

A scrutiny of recent volumes of this journal and of the British journal *Educational Research* shows no signs of a change in the concerns of educational researchers. Of some 50 articles published in *Educational Research* in vols 17 and 18 (1974–5 and 1975–6) none were directly critical of accepted research paradigms. Apart from the article cited above, the *American Educational Research Journal* in vols 11 and 12 (1974 and 1975) carried only two articles (out of a total of about 70) which examined conventional research methodology in ways that implied it might be inappropriate to the needs of the field. One of these considered the relation of research to policy, but without any deep examination of the implications of the relationship for the philosophy of educational research, and the other complained of 'abuse of the linear model' – again without pushing the critique to any fundamental level. 'Evaluation of Published Educational Research: a national survey', an article which appears in volume 12, assumes that there is no need to examine the question of whether the traditional criteria of research are defensible, and proceeds to report judgments of articles against a totally conventional paradigm in the 'reconstructed logic of science' tradition (A. W. Ward *et al.*, *American Educational Research Journal*, 12, 1975, pp. 109–28).

On the other hand, in the four years 1973–6, just over 15 per cent of articles in the *Journal of Curriculum Studies* expressed criticism of curriculum theory or research methodologies, or suggested new ways of looking at curriculum problems and tasks (see, for example, Walker, op. cit., F. Inglis, 'Ideology and the curriculum: the value assumptions of system builders', 6, 1974, pp. 3–14, George H. Willis, 'Curriculum criticism and literary criticism', 7, 1975, pp. 3–17, David Soulsby, 'Gagné's hierarchical theory of learning: some conceptual difficulties', 7, 1975, pp. 122–32 or Carl Parsons, 'The new evaluation: a cautionary note', 8, 1976, pp. 125–38).

15 Department of Health, Education and Welfare, *Urban School Crisis: The Problems and Solutions*, quoted in Harry Passow, 'Urban education: the new challenge', Invited Address, American Educational Research Association Meeting, New York, 1977, p. 10.

16 For a fuller discussion of the nature of curriculum problems, see Chapter 4.

17 Walker, op. cit., p. 59.

18 D. F. Walker, 'A naturalistic model for curriculum development', *School Review*, 80, 1971, pp. 56–65.

19 R. W. Tyler, *Basic Principles of Curriculum and Instruction*, University of Chicago Press, 1949. H. Taba, *Fundamentals of Curriculum Development*, New York, Harcourt Brace, 1962.

20 Walker, op. cit., 1973, p. 70.

21 Ibid., p. 59, Walker's remark relates to what he terms 'empirical research in curriculum', the definition of which excludes 'the activities of creating curriculum materials, curriculum planning and policy-making, the implementation of curriculum plans and policies and the criticism of existing, past, or proposed curricula' (p. 60). Such sweeping exclusions seem to contradict his desire that research should respond to the central questions of what should be taught, studied or learned. Powerful arguments are made for a redirection of curriculum research, yet the changes actually advocated seem far from fundamental. The reasons for this are difficult to see. If the field is defined by its problems, why should we admit or reject particular kinds of research according to a criterion of 'empiricism'?

22 M. Parlett and D. Hamilton, 'Evaluation as illumination: a new approach to the study of innovatory programmes', in Tawney, op. cit., pp. 84–101.

23 This view is advocated by, for example, Stenhouse (L. Stenhouse, *An Introduction to Curriculum Research and Development*, London, Heinemann, 1975). The present argument is that curriculum research should be conducted within a framework of action, but this is not the same as saying that all that is done within a framework of action is therefore research. To see development as research may be at the present time heuristically good for curriculum developers in giving them more appropriate attitudes towards their role, but it is very doubtful if the argument can be made to work the other way round.

24 W. A. Reid, 'What is curriculum research?' in P. H. Taylor and J. Walton (eds), *The Curriculum: Research, Innovation and Change*, London, Ward Lock, 1973, pp. 92–3.

25 Walker, op. cit., 1973.

26 D. F. Walker, 'Curriculum development in an art project' in W. A. Reid and D. F. Walker, *Case Studies in Curriculum Change: Great Britain and the United States*, London, Routledge & Kegan Paul, 1975, pp. 91–135.

27 Studies have, however, been carried out in other areas of political and judicial decision-making. See, for example, D. W. Rohde and H. J. Spaeth, *Supreme Court Decision-Making*, San Francisco, Freeman, 1976, and R. A. Bauer, I. de Sola Pool and L. A. Dexter, *American Business and Public Policy: The Politics of Foreign Trade*, New York, Atherton, 1963.

28 *Times Educational Supplement*, 20 May 1977, p. 13, 'New maths: raising more problems than it solves'.

29 E. W. Eisner, 'The perceptive eye: toward the reformation of educational evaluation', Invited Address, American Educational Research Association Meeting, Washington, DC, 1975.

30 As Eisner points out, teachers naturally deal in intuitive judgments of the quality of classrooms and schools when curriculum tasks are under discussion.

31 Ibid., pp. 18 and 20.

32 Ibid., p. 14.

33 A. B. Hodgetts, *What Culture? What Heritage? A Study of Civic Education in Canada*, Toronto, Ontario Institute for Studies in Education, 1972.

34 See, for example, the research appendices to the Plowden Report (Central Advisory Council for Education (England), *Children and their Primary Schools*, 2 vols, London, HMSO, 1967).

35 G. Vickers, *Value Systems and Social Process*, London, Tavistock, 1968, p. 113.

36 For this reason, a simple extension of the methods of behavioural research into areas of relevance to curriculum decision-making does not answer the need for curriculum research. The question 'what kinds of teaching methods lead to higher gains on standardised tests?' is not only an inappropriate one for research cast within a correlational paradigm, it is also unhelpful to decision-makers. (For a recent example of research

of this type, see N. Bennett *et al.*, *Teaching Styles and Pupil Progress*, London, Open Books, 1976.)

37 For elaboration of these points, see Chapter 5.

38 Parlett and Hamilton, op. cit. R. E. Stake, 'An approach to the evaluation of instructional programs (program portrayal versus analysis)', paper delivered at the American Educational Research Association Meeting, Chicago, 1972.

39 Schools Council, *Evaluation in Curriculum Development: Twelve Case Studies*, London, Macmillan, 1973.

40 Central Advisory Council for Education (England), op. cit.

41 The 'national debate' in England on the school curriculum, launched in 1976, was accompanied by the production of a series of papers from the Department of Education and Science under the general title of 'matters for discussion'. It cannot be said that they make a serious contribution either to a general awareness of the nature of curriculum problems, or to our ability to solve particular problems. They are, for the most part, a blend of pious hopes, conventional wisdom and sometimes interesting, but usually unassimilated data (DES, *Ten Good Schools: a Secondary School Enquiry*, HMI Series, Matters for Discussion 1; *Classics in Comprehensive Schools*, Matters for Discussion 2; *Modern Languages in Comprehensive Schools*, Matters for Discussion 3, London, HMSO, 1977).

42 See, for example, P. H. Taylor *et al.*, *The English Sixth Form: A Case Study in Curriculum Research*, London, Routledge & Kegan Paul, 1974 and P. H. Taylor *et al.*, *Purpose, Power and Constraint in the Primary School Curriculum*, Schools Council Research Studies, London, Macmillan, 1974. Many topics germane to curriculum problem solving are left untouched by these studies, but they do address some of the needs for data relevant to the carrying out of curriculum tasks in the particular areas of education they deal with. The findings, particularly on sixth form curriculum, render the failure of the Council to make progress on curriculum questions entirely predictable.

43 This view of the nature of curriculum tasks is due to the evaluation model proposed by Stake in his 1967 article 'The countenance of curriculum evaluation', *Teachers' College Record*, 68, pp. 523–40 (see also Reid, op. cit., pp. 93–5).

44 This question is further pursued in Chapter 4.

Chapter 4 Practical reasoning and curriculum decisions

1 An alternative view is that expressed by Kallós and Lundgren: 'Curriculum studies cannot primarily be focussed on *how* a curriculum should be constructed or developed, but must primarily explain the determinants of the curriculum' (D. Kallós and U. P. Lundgren, 'An enquiry concerning curriculum: foundations for curriculum change', Pedagogiska Institutionen, University of Gothenburg, mimeo., 1976). Much hinges on the meaning of the word 'primarily'. If what is being said is that an understanding of how a curriculum can change must precede any attempt to change it, then there is no serious disagreement

with the position taken in the present paper. It seems more likely, however, that what is being claimed is that the major focus of curriculum studies should be on the theoretic rather than the practical. If so, it has to be shown that the social and political determinants of the curriculum are significantly different from those that shape other human activities. If they are not, then their study should form part of the social sciences generally. Any significant uniqueness of curriculum as an activity is more likely to lie in the tasks it proposes than in the forces that determine its nature.

2 J. J. Schwab, 'The practical: a language for curriculum', *School Review*, 78, 1969, pp. 1–24. For a philosophical discussion of 'uncertain practical questions', see D. P. Gauthier, *Practical Reasoning: The Structure and Foundations of Prudential and Moral Arguments and their Exemplification in Discourse*, Oxford University Press, 1963.

3 Gauthier, op. cit., pp. 1 and 49.

4 'Where logic and strategy have received large and successful study down the ages, yielding the most powerful canons and instructions for their use, the more particular arts of deliberation and tactics have been given little more than honor for their function. From Aristotle to Dewey and Pierce, they have been recognised for what they do, honored for their contribution to our lives, but given little or no attention in their own right' (J. J. Schwab, foreword to W. A. Reid and D. F. Walker, *Case Studies in Curriculum Change: Great Britain and the United States*, London, Routledge & Kegan Paul, 1975, p. viii).

5 Gauthier, op. cit., p. 24.

6 Powerful arguments have been made on moral grounds against the supposition that ends can justify means. '(T)o manipulate men, to propel them towards goals which you – the social reformer – see, but they may not, is to deny them their human essence, to treat them as objects without wills of their own, and therefore to degrade them' (Isaiah Berlin, *Two Concepts of Liberty*, Oxford University Press, 1958, p. 22). These are matters of faith and feeling on which the curriculum theorist should declare his position.

7 See, for example, A. Kotov, *Think like a Grandmaster*, London, Batsford, 1971.

8 And confusion can be deeper still. What are we to make of 'a curriculum theory ought to be a rational explanation of why a certain content shall be taught and why activities shall be used'? (U. P. Lundgren, *Frame Factors and the Teaching Process: A Contribution to Curriculum Theory and Theory on Teaching*, Stockholm, Almqvist & Wiksell, 1972, p. 38). Is this a question about prudential action or theoretic understanding?

9 I am indebted to Ian Westbury for this conception of Tyler's contribution to curriculum theory. As I have said elsewhere, 'Tyler's work was more important for the logical extensions which it invited than for what it specifically recommended, and for what was conspicuously omitted than for what was included' (Reid and Walker, op. cit., p. 243).

10 D. Reisman, N. Glazer and R. Denney, *The Lonely Crowd*, New Haven, Conn., Yale University Press, 1950.

11 See, D. McKie, *A Sadly Mismanaged Affair: A Political History of the Third London Airport*, London, Croom Helm, 1973.
12 R. McKeon, 'Philosophy and action', *Ethics*, 62, 1952, p. 84.
13 D. Bell, *The Coming of Post-Industrial Society: A Venture in Social Forecasting*, London, Heinemann, 1974, p. 336.
14 S. Hampshire, *Thought and Action*, London, Chatto & Windus, 1959, p. 151. Cf. also, 'there is no way of considering the nature and quality of the act intended except by comparing it with more and more groups of other actions, and by describing it in different terms and by drawing attention to different features of the surrounding situation' (p. 218), and 'One does not in general need to consider the occasion on which a belief was formed in somebody's mind in order to decide upon its truth, in the same way that one generally needs to consider the occasion upon which an action was performed in order to decide upon its rightness' (p. 150).
15 See, for example, K. R. Popper, *Objective Knowledge: An Evolutionary Approach*, Oxford University Press, 1972, Chapter 2 ('Science, philosophy, rational thought, must all start from common sense' (p. 33)).
16 McKeon, op. cit., p. 79.
17 De Groot was able to show through empirical research that, although players at the master level tended to analyse more deeply, they were less likely than grandmasters to find the best move in a given position (A. D. de Groot, *Thought and Choice in Chess*, The Hague, Mouton, 1965).
18 I. Scheffler, 'Justifying curriculum decisions', *School Review*, 56, 1958, pp. 461–72 (reprinted in I. Scheffler, *Reason and Teaching*, London, Routledge & Kegan Paul, 1973, pp. 115–25).
19 Ibid., p. 116.
20 M. Shipman, *Inside a Curriculum Project*, London, Methuen, 1974. L. M. Smith and P. M. Keith, *Anatomy of Educational Innovation: An Organisational Analysis of an Elementary School*, New York, Wiley, 1971.
21 Deliberation on open education reached a remarkable peak in England in the various enquiries, reports and books on the 'William Tyndale affair'. See, for example, J. Gretton and M. Jackson, *William Tyndale: Collapse of a School or a System?*, London, Allen & Unwin, 1976.
22 J. J. Schwab, 'The practical 3: translation into curriculum', *School Review*, 81, 1973, pp. 501–22.
23 Hampshire, op. cit., p. 105 and Gauthier, op. cit., p. 4.
24 Schwab, op. cit., 1973, p. 515.
25 Ibid., p. 519.
26 See, for example, S. Fox, 'A practical image of the practical', *Curriculum Theory Network*, no. 10, Fall 1972, pp. 45–57 and E. H. Hegarty, 'The problem identification phase of curriculum deliberation: use of the nominal group technique', *Journal of Curriculum Studies*, 9, 1977, pp. 31–41.
27 D. F. Walker, 'Curriculum development in an art project', in Reid and Walker, op. cit., pp. 91–135.
28 Ibid., p. 92.
29 The studies that have been made of working groups have (1) tended to direct attention towards general rather than specialist problem solving and (2) have often used specially constituted rather than already

established groups. There is a need for more studies of the Walker type which take actual working groups and look at them in terms of the unique features of the curriculum tasks they have to carry out (see R. F. Bales, *Interaction Process Analysis: A Method for the Study of Small Groups*, Cambridge, Mass., Addison-Wesley, 1951 and J. E. McGrath and I. Altman, *Small Group Research – a Synthesis and Critique of the Field*, New York, Holt, Rinehart, 1966).

30 Walker, op. cit., p. 92.

31 *New Scientist*, vol. 68, 11 December 1975, pp. 648–9 and vol. 72, 4 November 1976, pp. 286–8.

32 G. Vickers, *The Art of Judgment*, London, Chapman & Hall, 1965.

33 Ibid., p. 28.

34 G. Vickers, *Value Systems and Social Process*, London, Tavistock, 1968, p. 146.

35 Vickers, op. cit., 1965, p. 62.

36 Just as in curriculum evaluation, those who are not satisfied with what one enquiry produces set up another. This has happened, for example, in the case of the NFER evaluation of the teaching of French in English primary schools which came to largely unfavourable conclusions.

37 Vickers, op. cit., 1965, p. 62

38 McKie, op. cit., p. 74.

39 For amplification of this point, see W. A. Reid, 'The changing curriculum: theory and practice', in Reid and Walker, op. cit., pp. 244–7.

40 According to Manzer, the growth of sub-governments is a feature of English political and administrative procedures generally. Stable relations develop among the interests clustering around a decision-making centre. The resulting sub-government then defends the *status quo* which permits its groups to pursue their objectives against limited competition while outside groups have to conform to the modes of behaviour established within the sub-government (R. A. Manzer, *Teachers and Politics*, Manchester University Press, 1970).

41 Schools Inquiry Commission (Taunton), *Report of the Commissioners*, London, Eyre & Spottiswoode, 1868.

42 Schools Council, Working Paper 53, *The Whole Curriculum 13–16*, London, Evans/Methuen Educational, 1975.

43 Ibid., p. 8.

44 Ibid., p. 17 (my italics).

45 Ibid., p. 8.

46 Ibid., p. 11.

47 Schools Council, *Enquiry I: Young School Leavers*, London, HMSO, 1968. This early report of research sponsored by the Council came nearer than most of their subsequent publications to providing the kind of data needed for deliberation on the curriculum. Though it is frequently cited, it was allowed to go out of print and did not establish a tradition of curriculum enquiry – possibly because the teachers on Council committees were sensitive about some of its findings.

48 Schools Council, 1975, p. 83.

49 Ibid., p. 106.

50 Ibid., p. 62 and pp. 64–6.

51 Ibid., p. 113.
52 Vickers, op. cit., 1968, p. 143.
53 See *Times Educational Supplement*, 15 October 1976, pp. 1–3, 'DES report to Prime Minister sparks off angry protests'.
54 Vickers, op. cit., 1965, p. 15.
55 Loc. cit.
56 McKeon, op. cit., p. 92.
57 See, W. A. Reid and B. J. Holley, 'The factor structure of teacher attitudes to sixth form education', *British Journal of Educational Psychology*, 44, 1974, pp. 65–73.
58 This project was set up in 1976, apparently as a political initiative and with minimal consideration of what problems it was to address or in what ways. The syndrome is described by Wise (A. E. Wise, 'Why educational policies often fail: the hyperrationalisation hypothesis', *Journal of Curriculum Studies*, 9, 1977, pp. 43–57).
59 *Times Educational Supplement*, 1 October 1976, p. 2, 'Justified impatience'.
60 Gauthier (op. cit., pp. 4–7) distinguishes between the 'solution' of a practical problem and its 'resolution'. The decision about what to do is a resolution, but the solution is an action. Resolution does not necessarily imply solution.
61 A. Kaplan, *The Conduct of Enquiry: Methodology for Behavioural Science*, San Francisco, Chandler, 1964, p. 24.

Chapter 5 The problem of curriculum change

1 'Ideology' here is intended to refer to any belief system, whether or not it is conventionally regarded as 'extreme'. Cf. R. G. Paulston, *Conflicting Theories of Social and Educational Change: A Typological Review*, University Center for International Studies, University of Pittsburgh, 1976, p. 3.
2 Bobbitt is taken as representative of the early 'curriculum management' movement around 1920 (see R. E. Callahan, *Education and the Cult of Efficiency*, University of Chicago Press, 1962). Historically Tyler links this phase of curriculum theorising with the more recent 'objectives-centred' phase associated with curriculum reform movements of the 1960s. See, for example, H. Taba, *Fundamentals of Curriculum Development: Theory and practice*, New York, Harcourt Brace, 1962, or D. K. Wheeler, *Curriculum Process*, University of London Press, 1967.
3 M. F. D. Young, 'Curriculum change: limits and possibilities', *Educational Studies*, 1, 1975, pp. 129–38. D. Kallós and U. P. Lundgren, 'An enquiry concerning curriculum: foundations for curriculum change', Pedagogiska Institutionen, University of Gothenburg, mimeo., 1976.
4 Critics of interventionism may admit that policies can be effective in delaying the time when certain social groups acquire power over what is taught. Moves to 'improve' the curriculum can always be represented as conspiratorial: 'the collision between the rationally founded movement of educational technology and the social liberal ideology have [sic]

emphasised the demand for measures whereby external control over the events in teaching are [sic] to be substituted by internal self-control. In practice this means a more subtle form of manipulation achieved via an increasingly invisible pedagogy' (Kallós and Lundgren, op. cit., p. 74). There are such things as conspiracies, but the demonstration of their existence should rest on empirical evidence, rather than on *a priori* ideological commitments. Educational events always *can* be interpreted as evidence of the manoeuvrings of power groups, just as individual actions always *can* be seen in terms of a Freudian theory of motivations. This is made possible by adopting a theory such that anything can be claimed to fit it.

5 H. M. Kliebard, 'Reappraisal: the Tyler rationale', in W. Pinar (ed.), *Curriculum Theorizing: The reconceptualists*, Berkeley, McCutchan, 1975, pp. 70–83 (reprinted from *School Review*, 78, 1970, pp. 259–72).

6 Ibid., p. 80.

7 F. Inglis, 'Ideology and the curriculum: the value assumptions of system builders', *Journal of Curriculum Studies*, 6, 1974, pp. 3–14. Wayne C. Booth, *Modern Dogma and the Rhetoric of Assent*, University of Chicago Press, 1974.

8 See, for example, D. F. Walker, 'Curriculum development in an art project', in W. A. Reid and D. F. Walker (eds), *Case Studies in Curriculum Change: Great Britain and the United States*, London, Routledge & Kegan Paul, 1975, pp. 91–135.

9 They may be effective in tightly controlled situations where techniques such as programmed learning can be successfully employed. Most curricula have to be designed to function as part of an 'open' system.

10 Young, op. cit., p. 130.

11 For a development of this viewpoint, see S. B. Sarason, *The Culture of the School and the Problem of Change*, Boston, Allyn & Bacon, 1971.

12 D. Silverman, *The Theory of Organisations*, London, Heinemann, 1970, p. 45.

13 In England, 'public' schools are independent (usually boarding) schools of high prestige. They are not state provided.

14 For a discussion of the grounds for considering that knowledge can be construed in this way, see K. R. Popper, *Objective Knowledge: An Evolutionary Approach*, Oxford University Press, 1972.

15 Marxists might claim that this is true only of 'liberally' inspired change that rejects revolution as a tool of innovation. But unless the revolution is to abolish schools (and most Marxists seem opposed to that), there is still a bureaucratic educational system to manage on the morrow of the revolution.

16 It is unfortunate that the word 'rational' has been unjustly claimed by theorists who believe implicitly or explicitly that it is possible to match the future state of an educational system to a predetermined plan. Rational action need not be so narrowly construed.

17 See, for example, H. Fallding, 'Only one sociology', *British Journal of Sociology*, 23, 1972, pp. 93–101, and R. Dahrendorf, 'Out of Utopia', in N. J. Demerath and R. A. Peterson (eds), *System, Change and Conflict*, New York, Free Press, 1967, pp. 465–80.

18 Fallding, op. cit., p. 94.

19 Ibid. p. 480. Paulston (op. cit., p. 39) says 'I view the functional and conflict interpretations of total societies and of continuity and change in education ... as dialectically related. Both views are necessary for adequate explanation of change and lack of change in social and educational phenomena and relationships.'

20 'The key concept bridging the gap between statics and dynamics in functional theory is that of strain, tension, contradiction or discrepancy between the component elements of social and cultural structure' (R. K. Merton, *Social Theory and Social Structure*, New York, Free Press, 3rd edn, 1968, p. 176).

21 The phrases are due to Fallding (op. cit., p. 100) and Kaplan (p. 428 in Demerath and Peterson, op. cit.).

22 For reference, see Table 1

23 For reference, see Table 1

24 C. Perrow, 'Hospitals: technology, structure and goals', in J. G. March (ed.), *Handbook of Organisations*, Chicago, Rand McNally, 1965, p. 915.

25 Ibid., p. 912.

26 P. A. Sorokin, *Social and Cultural Dynamics*, New York, American Book Co., 4 vols, 1938, vol. 4, p. 46.

27 See, for example, C. Jencks *et al.*, *Inequality*, New York, Basic Books, 1972.

28 For some examples, see N. B. Dickinson, 'The head teacher as innovator: a study of an English school district' and D. Hamilton, 'Handling innovation in the classroom: two Scottish examples', in Reid and Walker, op. cit., pp. 136–78 and 179–207.

29 For a rather more dramatic instance involving the whole technology of the school, see L. M. Smith and P. M. Keith, *Anatomy of Educational Innovation: An Organisational Analysis of an Elementary School*, New York, Wiley, 1971.

30 The problem of the growth of 'remedial' classes in comprehensive schools is discussed in D. Kallós and U. P. Lundgren, 'Lessons from a comprehensive school system for curriculum theory and research', *Journal of Curriculum Studies*, 9, 1977, pp. 3–20.

31 For a discussion of the extent to which the technology of the classroom is adaptable, see I. Westbury, 'Conventional classrooms, "open" classrooms and the technology of teaching', *Journal of Curriculum Studies*, 5, 1973, pp. 99–121.

32 D. A. Schon, *The Displacement of Concepts*, London, Tavistock, 1963, pp. 173–4 and 176. Compare Popper's discussion of the 'bucket' theory of knowledge (Popper, op. cit., pp. 341ff.), and also Chapter 2, p. 21.

33 Medawar points out that Victorian examination questions in zoology at University College, London, 'called for nothing more than a voluble pouring forth of factual information', quoting as an example:

> By what special structures are bats enabled to fly through the air? and how do the galeopitheci, the pteromys, the petaurus, and the petauristae support themselves in that light element? Compare the structure of the wing of the bat with that of the bird, and with that of the extinct pterodactyl: and explain the structures by which the cobra expands its neck, and the saurian dragon flies through the atmosphere. ...

This question, not the longest of the eight set in 1860, goes on for a further sixteen lines (P. B. Medawar, *The Art of the Soluble*, London, Methuen, 1967, pp. 114–15).

34 See D. Layton, *Science for the People: The Origins of the School Science Curriculum in England*, London, Allen & Unwin, 1973.

35 For a discussion, see P. J. Fensham, 'Science curricula and the organisation of secondary schooling', *Journal of Curriculum Studies*, 6, 1974, pp. 61–72.

36 W. J. Cheverst, 'The role of the metaphor in educational thought: an essay in content analysis', *Journal of Curriculum Studies*, 4, 1972, pp. 71–82.

37 Probably the most famous or infamous example is Summerhill at Leiston in Essex, founded by the late A. S. Neill. For a general discussion of 'progressive' schools which have deliberately set out to go against majority views on how education should be conducted, see R. Skidelsky, *English Progressive Schools*, Harmondsworth, Penguin, 1969.

38 R. Mandel, 'Children's books: mirrors of social development', *Elementary School Journal*, 64, 1964, pp. 190–9.

39 Ibid., p. 193.

40 Ibid., pp. 197 and 199.

41 Edward Thring, *Education and School*, Cambridge, Macmillan, 1864, p. 118.

42 See, J. Gretton and M. Jackson, *William Tyndale: Collapse of a School – or a System?*, London, Allen & Unwin, 1976, and compare L. Berg, *Risinghill: Death of a Comprehensive School*, Harmondsworth, Penguin, 1968.

43 The succession of models which inspired notions of 'liberal' education in England is analysed by Rothblatt (S. Rothblatt, *Tradition and Change in English Liberal Education: An Essay in History and Culture*, London, Faber & Faber, 1976).

44 See page 79.

45 S. Rothblatt, *The Revolution of the Dons: Cambridge and Society in Victorian England*, London, Faber & Faber, 1968, p. 53.

46 Compare the arguments in A. E. Wise, 'Why educational policies often fail: the hyperrationalisation hypothesis', *Journal of Curriculum Studies*, 9, 1977, pp. 43–57.

47 For an argument in favour of gradualism as a general approach to the planning of educational change, see Smith and Keith, op. cit., pp. 370–3.

48 Kallós and Lundgren show that, even in the apparently thorough planning of comprehensive reforms in Sweden, administrative arrangements were given more attention than the forms of the curriculum, which continued to embody many of the models derived from the old selective secondary school. This may have been due to conspiratorial action on the part of those who stood to preserve influence and power thereby: equally, it may have been due to a lack of vision and knowledge on the part of planners who were committed to the goals of comprehensive education (Kallós and Lundgren, 'Lessons from a comprehensive school system for curriculum theory and research', op. cit.).

Chapter 6 Rationalism or humanism? The future of Curriculum Studies

1 The word 'field' is not being used in any technical sense to distinguish it from 'discipline' in the way that it is used by Hirst (P. H. Hirst, 'Liberal education and the nature of knowledge', in R. D. Archambault (ed.), *Philosophical Analysis and Education*, London, Routledge & Kegan Paul, 1965). The relation of Curriculum Studies to the 'field or discipline' problem is one of many relevant issues which are not pursued here. For a discussion, see I. Westbury and W. Steimer, 'Curriculum: a discipline in search of its problems', *School Review*, 79, 1971, pp. 243–68.

2 W. Goodsell, *The Conflict of Naturalism and Humanism*, New York, Teachers' College Press, 1910, p. 3.

3 See, for example, R. E. Callahan, *Education and the Cult of Efficiency*, University of Chicago Press, 1962.

4 W. Pinar, preface to W. Pinar (ed.), *Curriculum Theorising: The reconceptualists*, Berkeley, McCutchan, 1975.

5 For a best-selling diagnosis built around the theme of 'consciousness', see C. A. Reich, *The Greening of America*, Harmondsworth, Penguin, 1971 (original edition by Random House, 1970). The 'new' consciousness is labelled 'Consciousness III' and is described as resting on 'respect for the uniqueness of each individual' and as 'deeply suspicious of logic, rationality, analysis and of principles' (pp. 211 and 216). Bell refers to it as 'a new polymorph sensuality, the lifting of repression, the permeability of madness and normality, a new psychedelic awareness, the exploration of pleasure'. The contrasting emphases on seriousness and pleasure are symptomatic of the basically conflicting assumptions of humanist and rationalist positions (D. Bell, *The Coming of Post Industrial Society*, London, Heinemann, 1974, p. 476).

6 B. F. Skinner, *Beyond Freedom and Dignity*, London, Cape, 1972.

7 *Saturday Review*, 22 February 1975.

8 R. W. Clark, *Einstein: The Life and Times*, London, Hodder & Stoughton, 1973, p. 247.

9 F. Inglis, *Ideology and the Imagination*, Cambridge University Press, 1975, p. 60.

10 M. Greene, 'Curriculum and Consciousness', *Teachers' College Record*, 73, 1971, p. 253.

11 Ibid., p. 266.

12 For a useful discussion, see D. Pratt, 'Humanistic goals and behavioural objectives: towards a synthesis', *Journal of Curriculum Studies*, 8, 1976, pp. 15–26.

13 Inglis, op. cit., p. 60.

14 R. S. Crane, *The Idea of the Humanities and Other Essays Critical and Historical*, University of Chicago Press, 1967, p. 67.

15 C. P. Snow, *The Two Cultures and the Scientific Revolution*, New York, Cambridge University Press, 1959, p. 3.

16 See, for example, J. A. Wankowski and J. B. Cox, 'Temperament, motivation and academic achievement: studies of success and failure of a random sample of students in one university', University of Birmingham, England, Educational Survey, 1973.

17 L. Hudson, *The Cult of the Fact*, New York, Harper & Row, 1973, p. 43.
18 Ibid., p. 16.
19 J. D. Thompson *et al.*, 'Truth strategies and university organisation', *Educational Administration Quarterly*, 5, 1969, pp. 4–25.
20 For an example of curricular utopianism in action, see L. M. Smith and P. M. Keith, *Anatomy of Educational Innovation: An Organisational Analysis of an Elementary School*, New York, Wiley, 1971.
21 K. E. Shaw, 'Paradigms or contested concepts?', *British Journal of Educational Technology*, 7, 1976, pp. 18–24.
22 Crane, op. cit., p. 12.
23 This argument is made by Walker (D. F. Walker, 'What curriculum research?', *Journal of Curriculum Studies*, 5, 1973, pp. 58–72).
24 Hudson, op. cit., p. 160.
25 H. A. Simon, *The Sciences of the Artificial*, Cambridge, Mass., MIT Press, 1969.
26 See, for example, F. E. Emery (ed.), *Systems Thinking*, Harmondsworth, Penguin, 1969.
27 G. A. Kelly, *The Psychology of Personal Constructs*, 2 vols, New York, Norton, 1955.
28 Herbert Spencer, *Education: Intellectual, Moral and Physical*, London, Williams & Norgate, 1861.
29 William James, *Pragmatism: A New Name for Some Old Ways of Thinking*, New York, Longmans, 1912.
30 'Reconceptualist' positions are too diverse for there to be any one shift in the focus of Curriculum Studies that would satisfy them all; see Pinar, op. cit.
31 Leading references are: J. S. Mann, 'Curriculum criticism', *Curriculum Theory Network*, no. 2, Winter, 1968–9, pp. 2–14 (also reprinted in Pinar, op. cit., pp. 133–48), and G. H. Willis, 'Curriculum criticism and literary criticism', *Journal of Curriculum Studies*, 7, 1975, pp. 3–17. It is not implied that writers of the articles cited in this or the three following notes are 'outsiders' trying to make a home in Curriculum Studies. On the contrary, they are, as I understand them, exploring ways of bringing about just the kind of humanistic trend within the field that is advocated in this essay. The point of drawing attention to their work is to illustrate the fact that the possibility of 'colonisation' by the humane disciplines is not such a remote one as it might at first sight appear.
32 E. W. Eisner, 'The perceptive eye: toward the reformation of educational evaluation', Invited Address, American Educational Research Association Meeting, Washington, DC, 1975. See also Chapter 3, note 29.
33 L. Stenhouse, Address to Symposium on 'The legacy of curriculum development and evaluation', American Educational Research Association Meeting, New York City, 1977.
34 R. Oram, 'An action frame of reference as a register for curriculum discourse', *Journal of Curriculum Studies* (in press).
35 For a brief discussion, see W. A. Reid, *The Universities and the Sixth Form Curriculum*, London, Macmillan, 1972, pp. 59–61.
36 For the shift of archaeology away from traditional modes of enquiry, see, for example, D. Clarke, 'Archaeology: the loss of innocence',

Antiquity, 47, 1973, pp. 6–18, or C. Renfrew, *Before Civilization: The Radiocarbon Revolution and Prehistoric Europe*, London, Cape, 1973. 'Inspirational' ideas, such as the view that prehistoric stone circles were astronomical observatories, have gained acceptance in recent years. 'Richard Atkinson wrote a splendidly trenchant review of ... *Stonehenge Decoded* ... with the delightful title "Moonshine on Stonehenge". In *Nature* Atkinson called [the] book "tendentious, arrogant, slipshod and unconvincing". ... However, ... arguments for at least some of the alignments are now widely accepted, and it is clear that Stonehenge ... was indeed an observatory' (Renfrew, op. cit., p. 222). It is interesting that giving scientific approaches a larger place in archaeology has made it *easier* for some theories originally thought of as 'inspirational' to establish themselves.

37 Crane, op. cit., pp. 158 and 168.

38 Reich, op. cit., pp. 252–3.

39 Walker, op. cit., p. 59.

Name Index

Subject Index